Praise for the *New York Times* Bestselling
Where the Light Enters

"Jill Biden's deeply personal new book, *Where the Light Enters*, will bring tears to your eyes." —*Parade*

"Her role as mother . . . is the undulating theme of her new book. Who she is now, in the wake of this loss [of Beau Biden], permeates this slender, often bold memoir. . . . This is not the typical memoir of a so-called political wife. . . . Such memoirs are good news for those of us who've always known that women married to politicians are more complex than the stereotypes of political coverage. . . . Nuanced . . . Biden is a model for how to build a new family without trying to erase the one that preceded it." —*The Washington Post*

"The lifelong educator shares stories of her life with husband, Joe Biden, in this often-poignant memoir that charts her journey from a rebellious teen to young divorcée to the Second Lady of the United States." —*USA Today*

"In this charming memoir, Biden shares an intimate story of her life with former vice president Joe Biden. . . . This generous and inspiring portrait of the Biden family is sure to be widely welcomed and enjoyed." —*Publishers Weekly*

ALSO BY JILL BIDEN

Don't Forget, God Bless Our Troops

WHERE THE LIGHT ENTERS

Building a Family, Discovering Myself

JILL BIDEN

FLATIRON
BOOKS
NEW YORK

www.flatironbooks.com

Grateful acknowledgment is made for permission
to reproduce from the following:

"Don't Hesitate," from *Swan* by Mary Oliver, published by Beacon
Press, Boston. Copyright © 2010 by Mary Oliver, used herewith by
permission of the Charlotte Sheedy Literary Agency, Inc.

All photographs courtesy of the author

Designed by Donna Sinisgalli

The Library of Congress has cataloged the hardcover edition as follows:

Names: Biden, Jill, author.
Title: Where the light enters: building a family, discovering myself /
Jill Biden.
Description: First edition. | New York, N.Y.: Flatiron Books, 2019.
Identifiers: LCCN 2019000561 | ISBN 9781250182326 (hardcover) |
ISBN 9781250182333 (ebook)
Subjects: LCSH: Biden, Jill. | Biden, Jill—Family. | Biden, Joseph
R.—Family. | Educators—United States—Biography. |
Vice-Presidents' spouses—United States—Biography.
Classification: LCC E840.8.B533 A3 2019 | DDC 973.932092 [B]—dc23
LC record available at https://lccn.loc.gov/2019000561

ISBN 978-1-250-18234-0 (trade paperback)

Our ebooks may be purchased in bulk for promotional, educational,
or business use. Please contact your local bookseller or the
Macmillan Corporate and Premium Sales Department
at 1-800-221-7945, extension 5442, or by email at
MacmillanSpecialMarkets@macmillan.com.

First Flatiron Books Paperback Edition: 2020

10 9 8 7 6 5 4 3 2 1

For my children:
Beau, Hunter, and Ashley,
you brought love and light into my life

CONTENTS

WHERE THE LIGHT ENTERS

PROLOGUE

A girl I barely know anymore stares out at me from a grainy wedding photo. She has feathered hair and wears a delicate tea-length white dress. She walks behind two little boys—frozen forever in their earnest jackets and ties—who already have her heart. As she approaches the stark, slatted door of the U.N. Chapel, her smile gives no hint of the journey that brought them to this day.

All these years later, as I sit on the big, soft couch in the sunroom in my home in Wilmington, Delaware, fragments of the promise made that day fill the room around me like a keepsake box—covering every inch of wall space with mementos, artwork, souvenirs, and pictures of our family.

The sunroom is one of my favorite places in the world. The small room overlooks the lake behind our house, and I like to sit with my feet tucked up on the sofa, wrapped in a throw, grading papers from my classes at Northern Virginia Community College, where I've taught English and writing for the last ten years. It's a room made for homeyness and comfort.

When I look up from the sofa, I see a photo of my daughter,

Ashley, and me. We're both smiling in that way that makes us look most alike, and it reminds me of all our similarities: our sense of humor, the candor we save for each other, our stubbornness. She gave me the picture for Mother's Day, printed along with a poem she wrote: "like the branches of a tree / I am an extension of you / my heart and soul / firmly and effortlessly / embedded in your roots."

There are posters from my husband Joe's Senate campaigns, and one from his 2012 debate with Paul Ryan at Centre College in Danville, Kentucky. It's in the style of a boxing match and announces, "Thrill in the Ville II." There's also a poster from my son Beau's run for attorney general of Delaware—always following in his father's footsteps.

A side table holds a photo of my son Hunter, captured when he fell asleep on the couch one afternoon. On his chest is his sleeping daughter, Finnegan, in a navy-blue jumper, her hair the delicate golden curls of a preschooler. Almost all of my pictures of Hunter are with his children, Finn, Maisy, and Naomi, and the frames can barely contain his love and pride for them. He's the heart of our family in so many ways.

There's a small paperweight of the White House seal, one of our mementos from the experience of a lifetime: eight wonderful years as part of the Obama-Biden administration. Not far from that is a candid shot of my parents, both gone now; a picture of my sisters, all four of them; and a formal portrait of four generations of the whole boisterous Biden clan.

On a wall nearby hangs a painting of a dock—the same dock that I can see if I open up the French doors just to my right. After Beau died of brain cancer in 2015, that's where I most often imagine him, with the ripples of reflected light framing his face. In my mind, he is looking out at the water in his Penn baseball cap or showing his kids, little Hunter and Natalie, how to hook a worm on their fishing poles. I would give anything to be able to go back to those days for just a moment.

When I put my feet up on the worn wood coffee table, I usually have to push aside a stack of Joe's daily media clips, a pile of student essays, or a box of colored pencils from the kids' visit. Natalie left a note taped to the mirror in preparation for our annual Thanksgiving trip to Nantucket that reads, "We can't wait to go to *Nana*-tucket!" It hangs next to finger paintings of cats and salamanders, an acrylic man, and a pen-and-ink blue-footed dragon—all original artwork from the grandkids.

The sunroom is where all the parts of my life meet: the career that has sustained my passions and independence for more than thirty years. The political adventure I never expected. The boys who made me a mother after their own was stolen away. The daughter who completed our family. The grandkids who pieced together the wreckage of our lives. The parents and sisters and in-laws and friends who helped shape the woman I've become. The man I've built this life with.

I am a mother and a grandmother, a friend and a teacher, a wife and a sister. Every scene on those walls, every role I've played, has taught me so much about what family means. I've learned—and am still learning—about the bonds that make up a family. Few of us would reduce those bonds, that gravitational force, to something as simplistic as blood. Families are born, created, discovered, and forged. They unfold in elegantly ordered generational branches. They are woven together with messy heartstrings of desire and despair, friendship and friction, grace and gratitude.

Strong love, we hope, is the mortar holding us together. Without it, we scatter like a pile of stones in the face of the inevitable: resentments, slights, betrayals, or just time. But love makes us flexible and resilient. It allows us to forgive the unforgivable. To become more than ourselves, together. And though love can't protect us from the sorrows of life, it gives us refuge. Inside its walls, we can huddle together and draw strength. Inside, we are always home.

This is the truest thing I know: that love makes a family whole. It doesn't matter if you're blending a family with biological and nonbiological children, or healing the wounds of losing a loved one, or inviting an aging parent to live with you. The details may differ, but love is the common denominator.

This is the story of how Joe and I created our family—through traditions, through laughter, through the simple ways we found joy. We had no road map or master plan. We faltered at times, but we never stopped working hard to keep the family strong. And we did it all together. We built our family, rebuilt it when we had to, and discovered along the way the meaning behind the beautiful words of the thirteenth-century Persian poet Rumi from the poem "Childhood Friends":

> Let a teacher wave away the flies
> and put a plaster on the wound.
> Don't turn your head. Keep looking
> at the bandaged place. That's where
> the light enters you.
> And don't believe for a moment
> that you're healing yourself.

1

FAMILY TIES

Every family has its own mythology—stories we tell again and again, until it's difficult to distinguish the colorful characters in our heads from the real people we know and love. These stories are true, or at least, they *feel* true. But they don't just record our history—they also illuminate the forces that shaped us and the values that continue to define us.

In my family, our legend was the marriage of my parents, Donald Jacobs and Bonny Jean Godfrey—two young starcrossed lovers, up against the world. And while not every tale needs a villain, every protagonist needs an antagonist—an obstacle to overcome. Fair or not, the legend of our family wouldn't be complete without its adversary: my grandmother Ma Godfrey.

I'm told Ma Godfrey could hardly hide her disappointment when I was born. There was no rational reason she should have been upset that her daughter—more than a year into her marriage—had given birth to a healthy baby girl. But despite my parents' wedding, despite the home they had bought and the future they were planning, my maternal grandmother still hoped against hope that they might separate. She simply believed that my father—who was from a poor family in Hammonton, New Jersey—wasn't good enough for my mom.

Having a child had, in her mind, sealed their fate together—and deep down, some part of my grandmother blamed me for it. Making matters worse, I looked like my father, with my blond hair and blue eyes. "You're not a Godfrey," she'd tell me. "You're a Jacobs." She might have meant that as an insult, but I took it as a compliment. Yes, I *was* a Jacobs, and proud of it.

Ma Godfrey's ambivalence toward me wasn't overt. She didn't treat me much differently from the way she treated my four sisters; she read me books and played the same games she played with all of us. She didn't withhold birthday cards or Christmas presents. But there was always an edge behind her comments. She was always a little faster to reprimand me, or to make a cutting, offhand remark. We all talked back at times, but I alone got a beating. Ma wasn't a warm woman, not with any of us girls, but her lack of affection seemed most pronounced with me.

When I was twelve years old, I'd had enough. I can't remember what she said to set me off, just that it was mean and unfair and made me absolutely livid. I decided I wasn't going to spend another minute with a woman who might love me but sure didn't like me much, so I called a cab company to pick me up. Luckily, my destination was just a few miles away.

My father's mother, Grandmom Jacobs, was the perfect opposite of Ma Godfrey. Every time I walked in her door, she would smother me in kisses. Her home was old and lived in and smelled like burnt Italian bread toast—a smell that to this day takes me right back to her kitchen. She always bought me my own cantaloupe for breakfast. She kept candy in the top drawer of the dining room buffet. And she loved us—all of us—fiercely and without reserve. When the cab dropped me off, she opened the door, pulled me inside, and wrapped her arms tightly around me. Safe in her grandmotherly embrace, I heard her whisper, "That *bitch*," followed immediately by, "God forgive me."

Maya Angelou once wrote, "Love recognizes no barriers. It jumps hurdles, leaps fences, penetrates walls to arrive at its destination full of hope." That was what my parents' love seemed to me: unstoppable, indomitable, and full of hope.

My father came from a working-class family of Italian heritage; his name, *Giacoppa*, had been changed to *Jacobs* when his grandfather, Guytano Giacoppa, arrived at Ellis Island. In 1944, at age seventeen, my father decided he wanted to fight in World War II. Too young to enlist, Donald needed his mother's permission, and though she wasn't keen on having her young son go to war, she signed his papers. He trained as a signalman and was sent to the South Pacific. Dad was very proud of his military service, and when he returned after the war, he took advantage of the GI Bill to attend business school in Philadelphia. He studied finance, which led to his first job in the banking business, working as a teller in Hammonton, New Jersey. It was a respectable job, but not the illustrious career my maternal grandparents had hoped would support their daughter.

A couple of times a week, Dad would stop by the Rexall Drugstore in town to order ice cream from Bonny Jean Godfrey, who worked the soda fountain. Today, their story seems too Norman Rockwell–esque to be real: the handsome young GI and the sweet girl behind the counter, the marshmallow-topped ice-cream cones and black-and-white tiles. And as in all good love stories, there was conflict: my grandfather, a pharmacist who owned the store, and my grandmother were determined to stand in the way of this growing romance. They watched the lanky young nobody from across the store, dismayed as he charmed their obviously smitten daughter.

My maternal grandparents, Ma and Pa Godfrey, had both gone to college, and they were determined their only daughter would do the same. Worried that Bonny Jean might decide instead to marry Donald, they forbade her from seeing him.

Bonny Jean did enroll in college courses, but she left within two years' time and didn't graduate. And she and my father never did stop seeing each other. Instead, in a secret act of rebellion unbeknownst to my grandparents, they sneaked away to Elkton, Maryland, to elope.

My parents continued living separately in their respective homes, and a year later they had an intimate wedding at Ma and Pa's home, with siblings and parents in attendance. My mother's parents went to their graves never knowing about the secret betrayal of their daughter. But it was a rebellion just the same, and it represented the pact of devotion my parents made to each other above all others. They created a sacred circle of loyalty that day, one that expanded with each daughter born—me, Jan, and Bonny at first, and then, when I turned fifteen, the twins, Kim and Kelly. My parents always had each other's backs, and they taught us to do the same. We might squabble with each other, but if anyone outside the family hurt one of us, they'd find all five of the Jacobs girls ready to fight back.

Every weekend of my childhood, my parents would pile us into our brown-and-white station wagon and drive us from our home in Willow Grove, Pennsylvania, to New Jersey to see our grandparents. We'd fly past the Nabisco factory, my sisters and me playing and arguing in the back seat. We'd ride past the row houses in Philadelphia, then across the Tacony-Palmyra Bridge, finally arriving in Hammonton. Once there, we split up: my father and I would stay with his parents, and my mother and sisters would stay with hers. I can't say for certain, but I'm pretty sure Ma and Pa Godfrey refused to allow my father to sleep with my mother in their home.

I didn't mind, because I preferred being at Grandmom and Grandpop's house with my dad. Grandpop loved to fish, and some days we'd come in to find dozens of rockfish spread out over the kitchen counters, the back porch, and even on the washing machine. I was mesmerized by their sleek, black, shiny scales, even as my grandmother screamed, *"Maledetto, Domi!"*—her nickname for *Domenic*. "Who do you think is going to *clean* all these fish?" She didn't speak Italian, but she'd made it a point to learn a few curse words for such an occasion.

My grandparents showed their love for my sisters and me through incredible food. It was at their house that I learned to appreciate pasta, homemade tomato sauce, and good Italian bread. My grandfather always sat next to the toaster, popping in thick slices of Italian bread and making sure we all had toast. The Italians have a saying, *"Finire a tarallucci e vino"*—to finish with tarallucci (little cookies) and wine. It essentially means, no matter our differences or our arguments during dinner, we finish as family. All's well that ends well—or at least, I think you're dead wrong, but let's put it aside so we can enjoy the pleasures of life together. That was Grandmom and Grandpop's home: a place where every meal ended with satisfaction—in our stomachs and hearts alike.

The kitchen was tiny, with a linoleum-covered table in the middle and leaded-glass cabinets along the wall. We spent a lot of time in that room, though I also loved their living room, where my grandmother proudly displayed a framed photo of my seventeen-year-old father in his navy uniform. It was a slightly ramshackle little house, and there wasn't a piece of new furniture to be found. But its features felt homey and welcoming, and my sisters were always a little jealous that they didn't get to stay there, too.

They'd be across town with my mom for much of the weekend, visiting the Godfrey grandparents in a very different kind of home. Ma and Pa Godfrey's lawn was flawless, with an embedded sprinkler system keeping the grass a perfect jade green; it even had a manicured rose garden alongside it. Ma had a collection of Hummel figurines arranged in a recessed bookcase, and a living room full of elegant furnishings, including an organ that she played with precision. She had an exquisite set of Lenox china, which my mother would later present to me with the words, "Promise me you'll never tell your grandmother I gave this to you."

Down in the cellar, shelves held perfectly arranged jars of peaches, pickles, and applesauce, which Ma made and canned herself. There was a freezer packed with ice cream, and a long wooden swing that hung from the ceiling. Even though it was a cellar, it always appeared freshly painted and absolutely spotless. Even spiders seemed afraid to trespass on Ma's domain. It was pristine, like everything else in that house.

At the end of every weekend, all five of us had Sunday dinner with both sets of grandparents. We'd start at Grandmom and Grandpop's house with a bountiful Italian feast: homemade noodles that Grandmom had hung to dry in the kitchen, braciole, meatballs, spaghetti, Italian wedding soup. The house would be suffused with the aroma of basil, oregano, fresh tomatoes, and garlic, and I could never get enough of the tastes and smells. We'd eat our fill, get wrapped up in Grandmom's warm hugs, and then head over to our Godfrey grandparents' house for Sunday dinner number two.

At Ma and Pa's, the table would be set with a crisp tablecloth, the Lenox china, and the good silver, and Ma would bring out platters of roast beef, mashed potatoes with gravy, green beans, and cake for dessert. Of course, we'd already stuffed ourselves with Italian food, so nobody really wanted to eat, but Ma would always press us to take one more slice, one more spoonful. These Sunday dinners were a time of family togetherness, certainly—but also of unspoken competition between Ma and Grandmom.

By the end of the second dinner, Jan, Bonny, and I would have upset stomachs and just want to go home. My parents would load us into the back seat of the station wagon, where Jan and Bonny would instantly fall asleep. But I liked to stay awake, to listen to Mom and Dad talking quietly in the front. Outside the car, the night would be black, but I felt comforted by the glow of the dashboard, the smell of leather seats, and the gentle murmur of my parents talking and laughing all the way home.

Starting when I was about seven years old, I'd walk up the street most days to wait for my father to get home from work. Working bankers' hours, nine-to-five, he arrived each evening at suppertime, and our routine was always the same. He'd pull his car over, open the door of the blue Ford sedan, and lift me onto his lap. I'd grab the steering wheel with my little hands, "driving" us back to the house while he worked the pedals.

I loved this tradition, and I felt immensely proud of my dad, so handsome in his dark suit, sometimes wearing a Stetson hat, and always smelling like Old Spice aftershave. This was the late 1950s, and we were a *Leave It to Beaver* kind of family; when we got back to the house, my mother would be busy cooking dinner, hanging out the laundry on the clothesline, or darning socks. My dad would settle into his favorite chair and read the paper or turn on the Philco black-and-white TV to watch the Phillies game. Sometimes, Jan and Bonny and I would pull up our little chairs, too, so we could watch with Dad.

Sunday dinners with the grandparents were elaborate, but our nightly dinners at home were a big deal in their own way. Every evening, around 5:00 p.m., one of us girls would set the table, and someone would lay out a clean tablecloth. Mom would put out flowers—freshly picked from our garden, never bought from the store—or a seasonally appropriate centerpiece. Candles would be lit, and we'd all take our seats—never officially assigned, but always the same. We had a rectangular table with six seats (until the twins came along, at which point we had to add a seventh) and my father sat at the head, in front of the fireplace. Traditionally, wives would sit opposite their husbands, but my mom hated to be so far away from my dad. Instead, she sat beside him, where they could touch each other's arms or playfully nudge when they disagreed. I sat at the other end, beneath a picture window that looked out on the backyard and the woods that lay beyond, while Bonny and Jan filled in the rest of the seats.

For all the care and thought that went into arranging our table, there was much less effort put into what actually went on it. While Ma Godfrey spent time trying to one-up Grandmom with dishes and desserts, she had never bothered to pass her excellent culinary knowledge on to my mother. Simply put, Mom was a terrible cook. Nearly everything came from a can or the freezer—which wasn't unusual for families of our time. We'd be eating Mrs. Paul's fish sticks or Campbell's Cream of Chicken soup mixed with white rice (our favorite dinner), served on a china platter, followed by a crystal dish of chalk-pink Junket custard. For the most part, we ate it and didn't complain—I didn't know steak came any other way than thin and overcooked until I had dinner at a friend's house and realized for the first time that beef could have flavor other than salt. Still, since we weren't allowed to leave the table without finishing our plates, there were a few nights I sat there well past 9:00, struggling to choke down the last bites of boiled hot dog and sauerkraut.

Ultimately, it didn't matter what we ate, because we did it together. We laughed and gossiped and recounted our days. Those were the moments when we got to share our lives with each other, and nothing outside of the halo of candlelight mattered.

I started Sunday dinners at my own home after I married Joe, knowing how important those dinners were to me as a child. We continued them as the kids grew up and through the eight years that we commuted, most weekends, back and forth from D.C. to Delaware when Joe was vice president. I like to think of the number of meals that have taken place in our kitchen in Wilmington—the stories we've told, the decisions we've made. The kitchen has a big table, but it almost never goes unused, even now that it's just Joe and me. There are always kids and grandkids dropping by, or friends and neighbors who can be convinced to stay for dinner. When staff come by to plan an event, we usually end up there at the table eventually, eating a good meal and catching up on everyone's kids or vacation plans. Even when we're just ordering sandwiches from the local deli, I get out the cloth napkins and light a candle. If we're going to eat, we might as well take a moment to enjoy it—and each other.

Until I was ten, we lived in a two-bedroom house in Hatboro, Pennsylvania, where Jan, Bonny, and I shared a room. It's funny, the things you remember: Our bedroom had a dark blue wall with little bumps on it—a result of frozen paint—and in the summer, when we were covered with mosquito bites, we'd lie on our backs and rub our legs on that wall to scratch the itchy spots. In the winter, we'd slip out of bed in our flannel nightgowns and pull our covers down onto the black linoleum floor, which was heated, to warm ourselves up. And every spring, a robin made her nest in the rose arbor outside our front door; eventually, we'd see cracked, light blue eggshells on the ground and know that her babies had hatched.

When my father got a promotion, we moved to New Jersey

for a couple of years, and then to a bigger house in Willow Grove, Pennsylvania, where I had a bedroom of my very own. No more sharing with my sisters—now I had my own double bed, with a headboard that had built-in bookshelves. I had a vanity, with a big makeup mirror and ceramic poodle lamps on either side, and I decorated my walls with pennants, including one from the Ice Capades. My sisters and I loved ice-skating, and in the winters, Mom and Dad would take us to Washington Crossing, where people would come from miles around to skate along the frozen canals.

I loved my sisters, but like all siblings, we got into fights. Being the oldest, I was always left in charge when Mom and Dad went out. Inevitably, Jan—just a year younger—would end up screaming, "You're not the boss of me!" And I would yell, "I *am* the boss of you!" Wrestling would break out, and it would last until I sat on Jan to subdue her or said something mean enough to shut her up. Once, when one of my sisters broke one of my beloved poodle lamps, I ended up chasing her around the house with the fireplace poker. I wouldn't have actually stabbed her with it, but she didn't know that.

Jan and I took turns instigating fights, but the most memorable was started by my mother. It was the summer after my sixth-grade year, and Mom had brought home a couple of bushels of fresh Jersey tomatoes. We were sitting around the dinner table when she picked up a tomato, smiled mischievously, then winged it at my dad. *Splat!* His shirt was a dripping mess of seeds and thick juice. I gaped in shock, which turned instantly to delight as Dad picked up a tomato and flung it right back at her. Then chaos: All five of us were grabbing tomatoes and flinging them at each other, howling as red splotches burst all over the room and ourselves. My mom kept a clean house, but it never stopped her from having fun.

My mom and dad laughing as they hurled tomatoes at each other is one of my favorite memories. It was the only "fight" I remember seeing them have, though I'm sure there were others, real ones that happened behind the scenes. I knew my mother's temper could flare on occasion, and Bonny swears she once saw my mom throw a plate at my dad, Frisbee-style. Marriage is work, and my family, like all families, struggled at times. But for the most part, my parents kept these challenges from us. They made sure we always felt nothing but loved.

As a kid, I used to love going to Pa Godfrey's drugstore, imagining my parents lingering at the soda fountain and chatting with each other across the counter in their younger days. But it was just as easy to imagine Ma Godfrey giving my father a dirty look from across the store as he flirted with my mother.

Ma wasn't great at showing her love, but I took it for granted that she did love me. On the day she died, I went to visit her in her home. There she lay in her bedroom on a hospital bed, with a hospice nurse by her side. I knew this was good-bye. As I leaned down to give her a kiss, the hospice nurse said, "Now, Mabel, give Jill a kiss."

And Ma whispered, "No."

"Ma, I know you don't want to kiss me, but I'm going to kiss you anyway," I said. I kissed her and left.

My feelings aside, Ma was a woman before her time—college-educated when few schools accepted women. She worked for fifty years as a teacher, and she wanted her daughter to be educated and independent. When I visited her as a little girl, she would take me to her school—an old-fashioned one-room schoolhouse where she taught kids of multiple grades. When she read to her kids, she was enchanting, and I saw how she pushed them to be their best. Many of her students were from poor homes, and every year, she'd collect coats to distribute, as well as knit gloves and scarves for those who needed them. I admired her generosity and the way she inspired her students. It was a lesson in teaching I've kept with me.

Ma Godfrey never did relent in her opposition to my parents' union, even after five children and many decades together. We all just ended up sidestepping her anger—even Pa, who secretly sent us little care packages filled with Lifesavers and chocolate candies. We were never allowed to let on to Ma that he'd sent them, because she was so set against helping my parents in any way. And though all of us girls ended up knowing that my parents had eloped, we knew not to reveal that to Ma in order to protect our father.

What's even more remarkable is that, in their later years, it was my father who insisted that he and my mother keep going every weekend to see both sets of parents. Mom would have been fine with skipping a visit to her parents every so often, but Dad insisted. And when Ma Godfrey was elderly and sick, Dad was the one who looked after her, keeping her books, making sure she had everything she needed in the house, and checking in on her regularly. My grandmother had plenty of money to support herself, because Pa had owned the pharmacy. But my father provided the kind of attentive, familial care that money can't buy—and that a lesser man might have withheld.

It was his own type of small rebellion, showing up for someone who could never have asked for help. Giving kindness to someone who hated you. Putting aside your hurt feelings or bitterness at rejection because the woman you love most in the world cared about this person. That was what family meant to him.

In *Adam Bede*, Mary Ann Evans, who wrote under the pen name George Eliot, wrote a passage that perfectly encapsulated the love my parents had, the love I desperately wanted for myself:

> *What greater thing is there for two human souls than to feel that they are joined for life—to strengthen each other in all labour, to rest on each other in all sorrow, to minister to each other in all pain, to be one with each other in silent unspeakable memories at the moment of the last parting?*

Through disapproval and conflicts, my parents had carved out a small piece of the world just for themselves. I can still feel their joy if I concentrate: the sounds of soft laughter in the front seat of the car while their daughters slept in back, my father wrapping his arms around my mom as she cooked, two dinner seats pulled up next to each other at the table to capture every single moment of closeness they could find. Their love, their loyalty, their unflinching devotion to each other—that was the small request I made to the universe: *Give me a love like theirs. Give me a family of my own.*

2

PUSHING BOUNDARIES

Still wearing my button-down shirt, pleated skirt, and tights from school, I stomped up the hill from my house and turned onto the road where a kid named Drew lived. I was a thirteen-year-old on a mission, though I wasn't quite sure exactly what that mission was. Not knowing who might be home, I began banging on Drew's storm door. He was startled when he saw me behind the glass but moved toward the door with all the cockiness of the eleven-year-old neighborhood bully that he was. He opened it, and, without thinking, I pulled back and punched him in the face. "Don't you ever throw worms at my sister again!" I shouted, and then I turned and ran home.

Bonny was just nine years old then. She was a quiet child, though she would grow into a bubbly, affable teenager, the head cheerleader in high school, and a member of our homecoming court. And while she was strong-willed with her family, a trait she shared with me, she was too shy to stand up for herself with the neighborhood kids. This boy Drew tormented her with worms so much that she had become terrified of them. She hates them to this day.

Holding my sore hand, I raced back down the hill as fast as I could and burst into the house, my heart thumping. Bonny was in the dining room with my father, who'd just gotten home from work. "Daddy!" I said. "I just punched a kid for throwing worms at Bonny!"

In 1964, not every father would be thrilled that his thirteen-year-old—his *daughter,* no less—had gotten into a fistfight, but my father beamed with pride. "Good for you, *Jilly-bean!*" he said. "That's the way to look out for your sister."

It's easy to idealize the past, especially when you come from a close-knit family like mine in the Philadelphia suburbs of the 1950s—the perfect cocoon for childhood. We caught fireflies on hot summer nights. We climbed trees too high and wandered through the woods unsupervised. There were no parenting books—at least none that would have made their way into the Jacobses' home—and, for better or worse, my mom and dad simply followed their instincts.

Child psychologists will tell you that children who feel safe—children who know they are loved and valued—tend to test boundaries more often. Compliance, it's sometimes thought, may be more a sign of resignation to a situation children feel is stacked against them rather than a sign of good behavior. Rebellion against adolescent gatekeepers, on the other hand—parents and teachers, seemingly arbitrary rules, expectations heaped upon them—can help kids figure out what they believe and who they are.

As the oldest of five girls, I was the first one to push the boundaries my parents set. I had a curfew of midnight on the weekends, which I would regularly break. And just as regularly, my parents would wait up, catch me coming in late, and ground me. Relegated to my room, I'd send notes back and forth with my friend who lived next door; our houses were close enough that we had set up a pulley system between our bedroom windows. She and I would send silly messages to each other, attached with clothespins to a string, and that at least helped pass the time.

When I was really restless for adventure, though, I'd sneak out late at night after my parents were asleep.

From June to August, the Upper Moreland Swim Club was the place to be for many of my friends. It was a refuge from the relentless summer sun for anyone who could afford the membership. That did not include my family or my friend Susan's. We could occasionally be invited as guests, but that only served to remind us that we were otherwise unwelcome in suburban teen paradise, so Susan and I decided we'd just break in.

On prearranged nights, long after midnight had come and gone, I would tiptoe down the steps and out of the house and walk a half mile to Susan's. She'd come out to meet me, and we'd walk another mile and a half to the swim club. With no streetlights, it was pitch-black, and we walked down pavement still warm from the day's heat. We hid at the sight of cars, lest some Good Samaritan (or kidnapper) felt the need to pick up two stray thirteen-year-olds. To get to the pool, we had to run across the multilaned Pennsylvania Turnpike, dodging cars going sixty miles an hour. Even now, I can't believe we did this—two young girls, out alone at 3:00 a.m., darting across multiple lanes of highway traffic. Once we got to the club, we had our final obstacle: jumping the towering chain-link fence.

But after that, the pool was all our own. For one joyous, splash-filled hour, no one could tell us what we couldn't do. Then we'd climb back over the fence and walk the dark trail home. My parents slept so heavily, they never found out—which is good, because I would have been grounded forever.

My father infuriated me when I was a teenager. He was the strict parent, the disciplinarian with the unenviable task of trying to keep five daughters in line. Whenever Mom got mad enough to yell at us, it was only a few seconds before we'd all end up laughing. But when Dad got mad, the yelling was real. He and I clashed most of all, not only because I was the oldest but also because he and I were so much alike: strong-willed, sometimes judgmental. We had high expectations for the people we loved, but most of all, we had high expectations for ourselves.

I often say that our fathers are our first heroes, and mine was no different. I wanted him to approve of me, and I worked hard to impress him. When I said I planned to go to college, he said, "Which one?" When I told him I wanted to go to graduate school: "What took you so long?" There were times when it felt like he expected too much of me. But when I ran my first marathon at age forty-seven, my father was the first person I called. It felt wonderful to make him proud. He didn't lavish us with praise, but when he said, "Good job," we knew we'd earned it.

My father and I loved each other, but we still quarreled regularly, especially during my teenage years. When he was really upset, he would call me a "cold fish." It makes me smile now, but back then I didn't find it so funny, so I found my ways to get back at him.

When my mother was pregnant with the twins, she paid me a quarter to do the ironing so she wouldn't have to stay on her feet. I'd dutifully iron all the clothes, and when I got to my father's undershorts, I'd reach for the can of spray starch, knowing he'd end up with a rash in unmentionable places. That was a satisfying revenge for a while, until my mother caught me and put an end to it.

I started smoking when I was about fifteen, and sometimes I'd do it up in my bedroom, sitting near the window and blowing the smoke outside. Both my parents smoked in the house, so I wasn't worried that they'd notice the smell. I hid my cigarettes and ashtray underneath my bed, where I also stashed my "dirty" novels. It was the perfect hiding place . . . until my father came into my room looking for something one afternoon.

I watched in horror as he crouched down to peer under the bed, then reached under and pulled out the ashtray. He stood up, looked at me, and quietly asked, "Were you smoking?"

"Yes," I said. He was too calm; I knew this was not going to end well.

"Come with me to the back porch," he said, and then he turned and walked out of the room.

I followed Dad to the porch and sat down at the picnic table, dreading whatever was to come. "I don't want you smoking," he told me. "It's a terrible habit." Then he handed me three cigars. "You're going to smoke these, and I want you to inhale them." I just looked at him. "Go ahead," he said, and I put the first cigar in my mouth.

On the first inhalation, I started coughing, my lungs rebelling against the thick, sickly sweet smoke. My father stood over me, watching with his arms crossed, and when I finally managed to catch my breath, he said, "Go on." I inhaled again, and once again my chest heaved with racking coughs. By the time I finished that first cigar, my lungs were on fire, my throat was raw, and I felt like I was going to be sick. And there were still two more to go.

Somehow, I managed to smoke all three of those cigars. But the instant I was finished, I ran upstairs to the bathroom and threw up—and not just once. I was so sick and miserable that my father started to feel bad. He came up, sheepishly knocked on the door, and said, "Come downstairs, Jill." When I didn't answer, he tried again. "Come on—we're ordering hoagies."

Hoagies! As if I were in any state to eat. As if I would give him the satisfaction of a conciliatory meal. Even if I had been able to eat a hoagie, I wouldn't have—just to spite him. Later that evening, as I slowly recovered and became increasingly hungry, I plotted sneaking food from the kitchen without my father noticing. But you couldn't have paid me to eat one of those hoagies. I went to bed with a stomach full of nothing but righteous indignation.

I also didn't stop smoking. It wasn't that I particularly liked doing it so much as I didn't want to be forced to do, or not do, anything. In my hardheaded rebelliousness, I refused to be moved by my parents' logic or reason. And once they realized I wasn't going to stop, my father gave in. "Okay," he conceded. "You can smoke, but only in the house." They didn't want fifteen-year-old me out on a street corner, a cigarette hanging out of my mouth. So we compromised. I kept smoking at home, quitting only after I got to college and realized I didn't have anything to prove by doing it.

Few people who knew me as that rebellious kid guessed that I would grow up to marry someone as steady as Joe. The political world requires a certain type of personality, and it's not one that has ever come naturally to me. Joe has always approached it with grace and dignity. He has built a reputation among political allies and foes alike as someone who keeps his word, who listens, and who can put politics aside to make progress. He's always been a statesman in the truest sense of the word.

This is one of his most admirable traits, but to be honest, his approach drives me a little crazy at times. We'll run into one of his colleagues, and Joe will be genuinely friendly and engage in conversation. As we're walking away, I'll say, "Joe! What are you thinking? Don't you remember the terrible thing that guy said about you last year?"

"No," he'll reply. "I forgot."

Joe has an incredible capacity to forgive, and he's incapable of holding a grudge. But that means that *I* end up being the holder of the grudges. I'm the one who wants to stomp up the hill to confront the mean kid. I remember every slight committed against the people I love. I can forgive, sure—but I don't believe in rewarding bad behavior.

In fact, I never did grow out of the stubborn determination I developed as a girl. I still hate being told I can't do something, though I've learned over the years how to stand up for myself rather than lash out in anger.

In the 1970s, being a senator's wife came with a lot of societal expectations. I was expected to stay home with the kids full-time and devote myself to Joe's career. I did stay home for a while, and I always supported Joe. But I knew from day one that I wouldn't be able to just live his life, so I went back to work. I pursued my education at night. It took me fifteen years, but I eventually completed two master's degrees—one as an education reading specialist and one in English—and then a doctorate in educational leadership. Joe used to joke that I did it because I was tired of our mail being addressed to "Senator and Mrs. Biden." And it's true, I did hate being called Mrs. Biden—that's Joe's mom's name, not mine.

Throughout my career, Joe has supported me every step of the way. I realized early on that teaching was more than a job for me. It goes much deeper than that; being a teacher is not what I do but who I am. I stepped away for a little while to be a full-time mom, but once I was comfortable that the kids felt safe and secure, I went back. I just couldn't stay away for too long, so when I told Joe I was going to pursue a full-time position teaching at Northern Virginia Community College (NOVA) after the 2008 election, he said, "Of course you should."

I've been told this was a historic first—that I was the only Second Lady to hold a full-time job while in the White House. Some saw it as a sign that I was a modern woman, while others said I didn't take the role of Second Lady seriously enough. But I never intended to make a statement. I just wanted to do the thing I love best.

So for eight years, counter to the advice of several senior advisors, I lived a double life: on Mondays, I'd go into the Eisenhower Executive Office Building of the White House, to an office with gleaming floors and marble columns, a stately fireplace, and floor-to-ceiling windows that looked out onto the grassy expanse of the National Mall. The next day, I'd go eight miles down the road to that small cubicle on the NOVA campus in Alexandria, Virginia. I'd alternate between worlds throughout the week.

There were times when it did seem ill-advised—nights when I had to wedge myself into the tiny nook beneath the Seal of the Vice President of the United States in the forward cabin of Air Force Two so that I could grade papers as Joe and I flew home from some out-of-state event. But I relished the tension of my life, caught between State receptions and midterm exams. Having dinner with the most powerful people on earth, holding study sessions with single moms just hoping to find their way to better jobs, scrambling into a cocktail dress and heels in the ladies' room at NOVA to make it on time to a White House reception.

I was grateful to be Second Lady. It was an incredible honor. But the role I have always felt most at home in is being "Dr. B."— working with first-generation college students, teaching them to write essays that would help them get into four-year colleges, helping military veterans see how the skills they learned in combat can be applied in civilian life. That was a deeper part of myself that couldn't be ignored. There was balance in the chaos that felt right. And I'm glad I was *stubborn as a cold fish* to make space for both.

While I butted heads with my father's disciplinarian parenting, my mother was always the person who made me feel safe to be who I was. She was the nurturer—not necessarily in a physical way, as she wasn't much for cuddling and hugging. But she was there for us in other ways, always ready to listen to our problems and fears. Mom was the least judgmental person I've ever known—a trait I wish I had more of. She understood that people had weaknesses, and her first instinct was always to help rather than criticize. In this, she was the complete opposite of her own mother; Ma Godfrey judged everyone and everything—just look at how she treated my dad. In retrospect, this was probably exactly why my mom swung so far in the other direction.

Since Mom was so trustworthy, my sisters and I always felt like we could tell her anything, and we did. Mom knew when I had my first boyfriend, she knew when other kids in the class started smoking marijuana (or *grass*, as we all called it back then), she knew when one of the girls at school got pregnant. There was nothing I was afraid to share.

Years later, there is no sound I miss as much as my mother's voice on the phone. Not what she said, but simply the notes, the tones, the rhythm of her sighs. Hers was the one call that could always calm me down; in my saddest, most frustrating times, just hearing her voice would get me through it. More than anything, I wish I had recorded her voice, but that's the kind of regret you never foresee. It's hard to know how badly you'll need something that seems small until it's gone.

But her love for all of us girls, and my father's love, too—in spite of our quarrels, or perhaps because of them—stays with me. It made me unafraid to push as hard as I needed to, to take chances and pick myself up when I fell flat on my face.

Winnie-the-Pooh author A. A. Milne once wrote, "One of the advantages of being disorderly is that one is constantly making exciting discoveries." From my adolescence to today, I have found that the disorderliness inside me has an important role to play—and that the discoveries I make as a result are almost always unknown pieces of myself. I'm so grateful my parents gave me the confidence and support to explore when I was growing up. The lessons I learned through that messy process, both good and bad, guided me as I plunged headfirst into the next uncertain and chaotic phase of my life.

3

CHILDHOOD'S END

Even our misfortunes are a part of our belongings.
—ANTOINE DE SAINT-EXUPÉRY

I grew up on *Snow White*, *Cinderella*, *Pinocchio*, and *Dumbo*. The lessons they taught me were straightforward: the kind and hardworking princesses always find their princes. The wooden puppet learns honesty and transforms into a real boy. The bullied little elephant realizes his own strength and soars into the spotlight, cynics and tormentors be damned. As I grew older, I would switch to adventure and mystery novels, like the Nancy Drew series and, my favorite, The Bobbsey Twins, where problems could always be solved with a little courage and cleverness. In life, it seemed, the world always moved toward righted wrongs.

These stories reflect what I wanted to believe: A world where life is, essentially, fair. Where good behavior and good people are rewarded. We tell our children stories that we hope will inspire them to be kind, to work hard, to do good in our world, with the assurance that when the book is closed, they'll live happily ever after. But not all children grow up on these stories. From Greek mythology to the story of Job, different lessons have been passed down through the generations, and they center on this idea: No one knows when tragedy will strike. Sometimes, for no apparent reason, good people fall and fail. Gods can take as easily as they give.

Perhaps if I'd grown up on a different type of story, I would have been more prepared for the world I found outside of Willow Grove, Pennsylvania. But I was raised on valiant princes and star-spangled banners. I believed that love conquers all, that justice would prevail. I don't think I was wrong—not in the long run—but I soon realized a lot of the details had been omitted.

It was a freezing Monday night in 1969 when a group of college friends and I gathered around a small television in a Newark, Delaware, apartment. We watched in nervous silence as men in dark suits took their places next to a big glass jar. One of the men reached in, pulled out a blue, pill-shaped capsule, and handed it to another man in a suit. He opened it, unfurled a slip of paper that had been tucked inside, and read aloud: "September 14."

For the first time since World War II, young men were being drafted to military service so they could join the fight in Vietnam. It was a lottery—those born on September 14 would be the first ones called up in 1970, with draft number 001. We braced ourselves as each piece of bone-colored paper was pinned to the bulletin board. The guy I was dating got number 042, and a couple of our friends were assigned even lower numbers. It was surreal to think of the lives wrapped up in those flimsy plastic capsules—they seemed too small to hold the future of so many men.

Even before I left my hometown, I was aware that the tectonic plates of our world were shifting. One Friday in 1963, my entire middle school filed onto the bleachers of our school gym for an announcement. We had a dance scheduled that night, which for middle school kids was a big deal, and I thought that was the reason for the assembly. When the principal announced in a solemn tone that President Kennedy had been shot, everyone in the gym fell silent. We sat there in quiet shock while the principal explained that the buses were coming so we could go home early.

For the next two days, the nation mourned as one. Businesses closed, and people cried openly on the streets. Most of America was transfixed by the coverage later that Sunday as the police led Lee Harvey Oswald through the basement of the Dallas Police Department. The Jacobs family was watching the coverage at Ma's house when Jack Ruby jumped out and shot Oswald in the stomach on live television. In that terrifying moment, the harsh reality of the 1960s made it past the walls of my idyllic childhood. And that was just the beginning; we would go on to lose Martin Luther King Jr. and Bobby Kennedy to assassins' bullets later that decade, and the deaths of these American giants would shake the country to its core.

Even so, our life in Willow Grove still felt removed from tumultuous politics—the protests and legislative battles, the rise of counterculture. My days revolved around school, Girl Scout meetings, cheerleading, and visits to the Dairy Queen. My mom and dad never talked openly about politics—though we knew they were registered Republicans. We saw glimpses of what was going on in the world in our newspapers, we heard parents whisper about drugs and rock 'n' roll, but on the whole it was background noise. Entering my teenage years, I focused on school, my summer jobs, and keeping my grades up.

But when I turned eighteen and started my freshman year at the University of Delaware, I suddenly saw the cracks in our society up close.

Like most Americans, my friends and I sat glued to the television coverage every night. We were the first generation to watch a faraway war unfold on the evening news. We saw the images of carnage on TV—napalm bombs, the My Lai Massacre, young soldiers being shot and tortured. We saw the flag-draped caskets. We hugged our friends good-bye before they deployed and felt their fear. We tried not to imagine the horrors they would see up close.

The war itself didn't take the life of anyone I knew personally, but one of my friends was shot—right here at home.

I was watching the evening news in May of 1970, when a special report came on. The Ohio National Guard had opened fire on students protesting at Kent State University, and four had been killed. As names of the dead and injured scrolled down the screen, I was shocked to see one I recognized on the injured list: Scott MacKenzie. *Is that* our *Scott?* I thought. Scott, from Council Rock High School? Certainly, he couldn't have been shot by our own National Guard. But a couple of quick phone calls confirmed that he was.

At twenty-two, Scott was a little older than I was, and he had been a peace marshal for the demonstrations going on at Kent State. So, while he was personally opposed to the war, he wasn't protesting that day. He was keeping an eye on the demonstration when the *pop-pop-pop* of shooting began. At first, he thought the Guardsmen were shooting blanks. Then a bullet hit him in the back of the neck and tore through his face.

Another student was able to rush Scott to the student health center, and he eventually made a full physical recovery. But his scars remained, just as our national psyche was forever changed. Outrage swept the nation. The resulting protests were so widespread that hundreds of colleges and universities across the country closed.

I had been raised to believe in the basic goodness of our country. But all I could see on the nightly news was callousness for life—for the lives of the men who were dying in a war that made no sense, for the lives of young people who were standing up to their government and asking for peace, and for the innocent families far away, caught up in geopolitical games. I don't remember any protests held on my campus, but I might not have gone if there had been. What, I wondered, would my voice add to this chaos? What would it mean to a government that didn't seem to be listening?

For all the frustration I felt about the war, I was grateful for the freedom I had at college. I traded in my conservative clothes for bell-bottom jeans and clogs and let my hair grow down to my waist—and so did some of the guys I dated. Suddenly, it seemed like none of the old rules applied.

The feminist revolution was well under way, and activists like Gloria Steinem and Betty Friedan were urging women to take charge of their lives. For the first time, my eyes were opened to the stark imbalance between men and women in our society. Very few women held positions of power, whether in the corporate world or in medicine, science, or politics. Women were expected to stay home, and those who did work rarely enjoyed the same salaries, benefits, or opportunities as their male colleagues. Women weren't even able to apply for credit in most places. I would see that discrimination firsthand when, for my first teaching job, I was offered a starting salary of $7,500 a year, while a man taking the exact same position was offered $10,000.

Even as a young girl, I knew that as much as my mother loved being a stay-at-home mom, it wasn't what I wanted for myself. My mother had been a straight-A student in high school, but she left college to devote her life to my father. It's funny, but I never once asked Mom what kind of career path she might have chosen. As far as I could tell, my dad and us kids were her life—morning, noon, and night. She might have had other ambitions, but we never knew of them.

After my dad left for work in the morning, my mom did housework and cared for us girls all day. She never lunched with friends or watched television shows. Reading was her only other passion; she could spend hours sitting and reading in the corner chair or doing a crossword puzzle—and she seemed content doing that.

I wanted a different kind of life. When I was a girl, I used to daydream over an ad in *Parade* magazine, which came with our Sunday paper. It was for Seagram's whiskey, with pictures of two mansions side by side. I'd look at them and imagine different paths my life could take. I wanted adventure, independence. I wanted to try on homes that were nothing like my own and see which one fit.

So I pursued my degree and planned a career—following,

in some ways, in Ma Godfrey's footsteps. At the University of Delaware, for the first time, I could see a path to that destination. Around campus, I explored what life might hold for me. I biked all over Newark, stayed out late at night, and met up with friends for drinks at the bars. As it was for so many young students, college was the beginning of my adult life, and I couldn't wait to see where it would lead.

The University of Delaware was a small campus then, and it was easy to make friends, as you'd see the same faces out and about. That's how I met a gregarious young guy from Wilmington, a student named Frank. He and I would say hi to each other, occasionally stopping to chat. It wasn't until much later that I took note of his last name: Biden. Frank Biden.

Frank is Joe's younger brother, but of course, at that point I'd never heard of Joe Biden. Joe was a councilman in New Castle County then, a local attorney who no one expected would run for Senate. And the truth is, I might not have noticed when he entered that race, because I had absolutely no interest in politics, apart from voting. I had never followed a campaign or taken a political science course—nothing. But, eventually, someone else became very interested in Joe's race: my husband.

The year I started college, 1969, the Rolling Stones released "You Can't Always Get What You Want," and I fell in love with a tall ex-football player who drove a fast yellow Camaro. The next year, we married when I was still eighteen. Looking back, it may seem like that relationship was a mistake of youth. But there was a time when I truly believed we were destined for each other. He was charismatic and entrepreneurial and eventually started his own business. We rented a sleek modern house. Suddenly, I wasn't just a student, eating cheap food and living in student housing any longer—now I was a wife. I shopped for two and decorated our home. My parents didn't object; in fact, my parents loved him. And most importantly, I thought I had found a love like my parents', a partnership built on loyalty and devotion. For a moment, we were happy. I had found my Prince Charming, and I was sure it would last forever.

My husband was much more interested in politics than I was and was a big supporter of the Biden for Senate campaign. In the summer of 1972, I started seeing Biden campaign brochures on the kitchen table. It wasn't just a long-shot campaign, it seemed to be an impossibility. Joe was young—in fact, he wouldn't even turn thirty, the legal age limit to *be* a senator, until after the election. He was running against the Republican incumbent, Senator J. Caleb Boggs, in a state where Democrats were rarely considered viable. His team wasn't made up of renowned political operatives but family, and his sister, Val, was running the campaign. He didn't have anywhere close to the funding his opponent did, and he kept missing out on fundraising opportunities with the traditional big-money players because he refused to promise them votes. In fact, at one point, he had put a second mortgage on his house just to stay in the race.

No sane person would have wagered much on a Biden upset, and yet he had a message that was resonating in Elk lodges and coffee shops and barbershops around the state. And he'd made quite an impression on my husband.

I was still going to school full-time, twelve to fifteen credits a semester, so I wasn't paying much attention to the race. What I wanted, desperately, was for the giant pile of Biden flyers to be cleared off our small kitchen table. But in November, Joe Biden shocked the political world. Up until the morning of Election Day, he was down in the polls—but by that evening, he had done the impossible and eked out a win by around three thousand votes. Even I couldn't help being a little caught up in the excitement. With the promise of a nice dinner afterward, I was persuaded to join the victory celebration.

The party was at the Hotel Du Pont in downtown Wilmington, an elegant historic hotel with marble staircases, terrazzo floors, and twinkling chandeliers. There was a magic feeling in the room, like a miracle had happened, and we were all the witnesses. People were packed in, celebrating and cheering. The crowd vibrated with energy, but it was all a bit too much for me—the noise, the emotion, the rising temperature. I was ready to leave for the promised dinner when I noticed a blond woman walking through the crowd, shaking hands and greeting people.

She had an easy, natural beauty that made her look almost out of place in the frantic crowd. Even surrounded by strangers vying for attention, she seemed calm, with a warm, genuine smile. From across the room, you could see how happy she was—happy, and incredibly proud. It was Neilia Biden, Joe's wife. On the spur of the moment, I decided to say hello. I walked up to her, held out my hand, and said, "Congratulations on your win." She took my hand, smiled graciously, and said, "Thank you so much." I didn't know much about her, but in that instant, I thought about how picturesque their family was—the handsome young senator, trying to better the world; his beautiful, loving wife, representing their family, always there to cheer him on; and three adorable kids. Here they were, with the world at their feet, taking on the political establishment and *winning*.

We didn't stay much longer at the party, as I was more interested in having dinner than hearing the speeches that were to come. I didn't meet Joe Biden that night, but meeting Neilia stuck with me.

A little over a month later, on December 18, 1972, I was listening to the radio while driving to campus to take one of my final exams. The announcer broke into programming to say that Joe Biden's wife, Neilia, and their thirteen-month-old daughter, Naomi, had been killed in a car accident earlier that day, on their way home from buying the family's Christmas tree. Their young sons, Beau and Hunter, had been in the car but had survived.

I barely heard a word after the news about Neilia and the baby. I pulled my car into the student parking lot and switched off the ignition. Neilia was gone, along with their little girl. It was profoundly unfair—to take a mother from her children; to take a daughter from her father. Joe Biden had had everything, and in a horrible second, it was gone.

Even after Joe and I were married, I couldn't imagine his pain. I couldn't imagine the devastation he had endured, losing so much and still finding a way to keep going. I sympathized, and I marveled at his strength. I knew the particulars: that he had felt he would never recover; the thoughts of suicide that were kept at bay only because two little boys needed him so much. But I didn't really understand—not until years later when Beau died. How could I? Grief like that is unknowable until you stare it in the face. Until it takes you apart and leaves you wondering how you can still look so much like the person you can only remember. You pray and pray to go back to before. You look for explanations. You wonder if everything happens for a reason. But it doesn't. There is no reason for losing a child, only days that keep coming and the people left behind who stand with you in your sorrow.

That cold December evening, life truly stopped for a moment, and I prayed for the Biden family. It was the only thing I could think to do.

My parents loved each other until they left this earth. Even in their old age, they were playful and affectionate. They loved faithfully and unconditionally. Marriage, for them, meant forever. And I knew, deeply, unquestioningly, that was what I would have as well.

So, when my marriage fell apart, I was lost. I watched, devastated, as it slipped from my fingers before I could even figure out how to hold on. We were young, and it didn't take long before we grew in different directions. It was at this point that I learned how essential it is to be financially independent, especially as a woman. My daughter would tell you that I drilled this message into her from an early age. Even now, it's one of the things I continue to stress to the women in my classroom and the young female students I mentor. That, and the fact that you can't always prepare for what life brings you. And in this instance, I was certainly unprepared.

I tried to make the relationship work. I thought I could will our marriage back to life. But I had to separate what I thought my family should be from the reality of what this relationship was. Before long, I began to see that the breaks were beyond repair. I wouldn't settle for a counterfeit love. Like a broken spell, the truth of the reality struck me suddenly: I was going to get divorced.

I'm not sure if I knew anyone who was divorced back then. The very idea horrified me. It meant failure, and in my still-young life, I had never failed at anything serious. I had let down my parents—especially my dad. I had let down myself. I felt ugly and inadequate; I was embarrassed and ashamed.

In a single devastating year, I went from thinking I had it all to feeling shattered and alone. I questioned if I would ever find love, if I would ever have a family of my own. How could I give my heart to someone again? How could I again risk this humiliation, this hurt? And how could I figure out who, exactly, I was?

I picked up the pieces of my life and tucked them away. My parents stood by me. They offered to let me move back in with them, but I said no. I wanted to continue to live independently. In my mind, my former husband thought I would disintegrate without him, and I aimed to prove him wrong. I decided to get away from Newark—away from the campus, the bars, and the biggest disappointment of my young life.

I rented a small place across the state line in Chadds Ford, Pennsylvania, about twenty miles from the university. It was a one-bedroom townhouse, modest, but just enough for me. I bought groceries for one. I smothered my sorrows in long study sessions and buckled down on finishing my degree. I dated men without hoping for much. I let go of fairy-tale endings, and I tried to reconnect with the brave person I used to be. I played my music loud:

> *You can't always get what you want*
> *But if you try sometimes you just might find*
> *You get what you need.*

4

A REAL GENTLEMAN

How did you get this number?" Those were the first words I spoke to Senator Joe Biden when he called me out of the blue on a lazy Saturday afternoon. It was March of 1975, and I had spent most of my morning running errands, so I wasn't expecting a call from anyone. Some people would have been excited to get a call from a senator; I was confused. I had unlisted my telephone number when I'd moved to Chadds Ford to avoid this very situation. Well, perhaps not *this* situation, but certainly one where I received phone calls from strangers.

"My brother Frank gave it to me," Joe said. "I just got back into town and was wondering—are you free tonight?"

Not only had I not expected a random call from Joe Biden, but I could never have imagined he would make that call to ask me out. I've been asked if I was starstruck by the fact that a U.S. senator thought I was worth a call, but I honestly wasn't. I was flattered that someone I'd heard of was interested. But at the time, I still wasn't 100 percent sure what a senator did exactly.

"No," I told him. "Actually, I have a date."

"Ah," he said. "Well, I'm only in town for one day. Do you think you could break it?"

It was a pretty forward request, but now I was intrigued. "Call me back in an hour," I said, and I hung up.

I had a date planned for that evening with a guy from Philadelphia. We had gone out a couple of times, and though he was good-looking and perfectly nice, I didn't expect anything serious to develop. I certainly wasn't looking for a long-term relationship. Still, I didn't want to hurt his feelings, so when I called, I told a little white lie.

"I'm going to have to cancel tonight," I said. "A girlfriend of mine just flew in from Washington, and we want to spend some time together."

"Hey, that's perfect!" he shot back. "I have a twin brother, so why don't we just double date?"

Well, that didn't work.

"Uh . . . I don't think she'll go for that. She's just in for the night, and we really need to catch up."

There was a moment of silence, and then, in a colder tone, he said, "Fine." I'm not sure if he realized I was blowing him off, but either way, I never heard from him again.

While I waited for Joe to call back, I thought about how bizarre the situation was. I didn't know much about him—mostly what I'd caught from the headlines over the years: winning the impossible election, losing his wife and daughter. I knew he was older than I and he had two sons. In pictures, he was always wearing a coat and tie, and his hair was short and clean-cut—nothing like the side-burned, bell-bottom-wearing guys I was used to dating. If nothing else, this would be interesting.

As I later learned, Joe didn't know much about me, either.

In fact, he had only sought me out because he'd seen photos of me at the Wilmington airport.

A few months earlier, my friend Tom Stiltz had asked me for a favor. Tom was trying to build a business as a professional photographer, and he'd signed a contract to shoot an ad campaign for New Castle County Parks and Recreation. He didn't want to shoot empty spaces, so he asked me to pose in a few of the pictures. It wasn't exactly a modeling job since I didn't get paid, but the blown-up photos ended up on display at the Wilmington airport.

And that's where Joe first saw my picture, as he waited for his brother Frankie to come pick him up at the airport on a Friday evening. At the time, he was flying back and forth from D.C. often—though later, famously, he would always take Amtrak—so he saw me quite a lot. When his brother arrived, Joe apparently pointed at the photo of me and said, "Look, Frankie. That's the kind of girl I'd like to date." And Frank said, "Well, why don't you, then? I know her." Frankie got my number from one of our mutual friends, and Joe called the next day.

After an hour had passed, Joe called me back. "All right," I told him. "I broke my date."

"Great," he said, "I'll pick you up at seven. What's your address?" And that was it—no chitchat, no pleasantries. We hung up, and I pondered what one might wear on a date with a senator. I imagined something smart and tailored, probably pearls and a skirt. Well, I wasn't wearing that. I settled on emerald-green slacks, a diaphanous flowered blouse with lace trim, and a pair of wedges. A couple of hours later, at 7:00 p.m. on the dot, Joe showed up at my door.

He was thirty-one and wore a perfect suit and leather loafers. He looked so straightlaced that the first thought that popped into my head was, *My God, what have I gotten myself into?* The second was, *Oh, well. It's only one date.*

"How about we go to a movie in Philly?" Joe asked. The press had taken a lot of interest in his dating life, as he was considered one of the most eligible bachelors in the country, and a night spent outside of Delaware would attract less attention.

Joe walked me to his car and gallantly opened the door for me. We set out for Philadelphia, getting to know each other on the drive up.

The movie we decided to see—I think—was a French film called *A Man and a Woman,* which, strangely enough, is about a couple whose new relationship is complicated by memories of their spouses who have died. Afterward, we went to a nearby restaurant, where we slid into a booth to have dinner. I don't remember much else about the movie, and I have no idea what we talked about, but, despite his appearance and dress, he was laid-back and funny. We talked for a few hours, there in the booth, and I was surprised by how easy and comfortable it felt. It was a much better date than I had expected it to be.

After driving me home, he walked me to my front door. "I had a really great time, Jill," he said. "And I'd like to see you again." I told him I'd like that, too.

"Any chance you're free tomorrow night?" he asked.

"Yes," I said. "I am."

He smiled, then stuck his hand out to shake mine. "Good night," he said, then turned and walked back to his car.

I went inside and closed the door behind me. It was 1:00 in the morning, but I had to talk to my mother. I dialed her number, and when she picked up, I said, "Mom, I've finally met a real gentleman."

The next evening, Joe and I had our second date, and though I don't recall where we went or what we did, I do remember that it was every bit as enjoyable as the first one had been. That night, after Joe drove me home, he did kiss me good night. And then he said, "Listen, I've got to work in Washington this week, but I'd like to see you again."

He pulled a little black calendar book out of his pocket and started flipping through it, furrowing his brow. "Nope, that night won't work . . . that one's booked, too . . . Gosh, this week is so busy." Then he glanced at me and said, as casually as he could, "Well, how about tomorrow night?"

Three dates, three nights in a row? *Buddy,* I thought, *you just blew your cover.*

5

IF YOU HAVE TO ASK

At that point in my life, the fact that Joe was a senator was low on the list of things that made our new relationship out of the ordinary. It's a demanding job, so scheduling dates was more complicated, and, of course, I had never previously considered what the press might say about my dating life. But in a lot of ways, working in the Senate was a job like other jobs.

The complication I found much more intimidating was his family—not just that he had children, though that was very new to me, but that the entire family was so close. Like my family, the Bidens prized loyalty to each other over almost anything else. Joe, Valerie, Jimmy, Frank, and their parents weren't just close; being a Biden was their identity. They were proud of it, and they loved each other fiercely. In fact, Joe's family has a saying: "My word as a Biden." It's a sacred oath; whoever swears to it has to be absolutely, 100 percent telling the truth. Even today, I'll ask my kids and grandkids, "Do you give me your word as a Biden?" If they do, I believe what they're telling me.

The fact that Joe had chosen Val and his brother Jimmy to play two of the most important roles in his campaign, and that he'd done it contrary to the advice of the party, was evidence of their bond. The fact that, against all odds, the family managed to pull out an impossible win was evidence of something else: that there was almost nothing they wouldn't do to support, protect, and fight for each other. That was especially demonstrated after Neilia's death.

The Bidens have another belief as well: "If you have to ask, it's too late." When someone is in need, when they're hurting, when they're overwhelmed, you don't wait until they tell you they need help. You give it before they have to ask. So when Neilia died and Joe was left with two young boys, trying to father them and get through his own grief, all while juggling the new hectic life of a senator, Val didn't ask if there was something she could do. She moved in. And for three years, through her own career ambitions, through her courtship and eventual marriage to her husband, Jack, she lived with Joe and the boys and made sure they had the love and support they needed to keep going.

Needless to say, the idea of breaking into that small, devoted circle was more than a little daunting.

"My sister wants to meet you," Joe told me one day, only a couple of weeks after we started dating.

Val wasn't just Joe's sister, he considered her one of his best friends, and she was the one I was most nervous to meet. By then, I knew Joe's brother Frank, of course, as well as Jimmy. Though Delaware is a place where everyone seems to know everyone else, and though I'd seen Val driving the boys in her Jeep a few times, I had yet to meet her.

I was intimidated. I knew Val was accomplished and beauti-

ful. In fact, she was one of the first women ever to run a successful Senate campaign. I also knew that her approval could
make or break my standing in Joe's life. She was understandably protective of him, and I was self-conscious about being the
new, young girlfriend.

So I just kept putting off our meeting.

Joe would ask, and I'd agree to go over to their house on
North Star Road to meet Val and the boys, who were then five
and six years old. But when the day came, I'd say, "You know
what? I don't feel like going tonight." Joe never made a big deal
of it—he knew it was a lot of pressure for me—but finally, after
having canceled four or five times, I realized I couldn't keep
making excuses.

So, one afternoon in April, I drove to North Star and parked
in front of a historic country house with black shutters and a big
barn out back. In the kitchen, Val and her then-boyfriend Jack
were busy putting a fresh coat of pale yellow paint on the walls
in preparation for Joe to sell the house. Joe introduced us, and
Valerie set about making us all tuna fish sandwiches for lunch.

She must have realized I was nervous, because as she handed
me a sandwich, she started goofing around. "Here's your tuna
fish!" she exclaimed, and then she started mewling like a cat.
"*Meow, meow, meow!*" she said as she pawed at my shoulder. It
was charmingly quirky, and her smile disarmed me. We both
laughed, me in spite of my nerves, and I wondered if I had
passed the test.

To this day, in addition to being my sister-in-law, Valerie is
one of my closest friends and most trusted confidantes. She still
tells the story of our first meeting—and we still laugh at the
"meow."

Joe's home was styled like a colonial farmhouse, with a sprawling porch along one side. We sat there eating our sandwiches while Beau and Hunter roughhoused on the grass. I didn't say a lot to the boys, but they were adorable and very sweet with Joe. It should have felt natural—the simple lunch, the easy conversation, the kids playing nearby. But even though Joe and Val tried to make me feel comfortable, it was hard to let down my guard. After an hour or so, Joe could tell this was enough for a first meeting, and as soon as the sandwiches were eaten, we made up an excuse to go.

Tragedy, upheaval, uncertainty—those moments in life where everything you know gets turned upside down affect people differently. For Joe, losing his wife and baby daughter, and leaning on his family to rebuild from the ruins of that fateful day, forced him to see the world with new clarity. From the heartbreak he had suffered, his understanding of family was deeper than ever. He had seen its power, through the longest nights, through the darkest thoughts; he had held on to these people—and, because of them, survived. Now, he knew exactly what he wanted and needed, and that was a wife and mother for his boys.

Rather than feeling sure about what I wanted, I felt nothing but confusion. I had thought I could recognize what family should be, and when I turned out to be wrong, when the illusion broke with my divorce, I grew bitter. I wondered if the type of family I'd dreamed of, a partnership like the one my parents shared, was even possible. I wondered if it was something I wanted at all.

In a lot of ways, I wasn't ready—not just for him but for *them*.

The boys were incredibly affectionate with their father, and soon with me as well. They were like puppies who always wanted to snuggle up and climb in my lap. They were constantly touching and connected to each other and to Joe as well, as if, at any moment, one of them could be gone. Joe had a nighttime ritual of gently scratching their backs and arms ("With your fingernails!" they'd insist) as they settled in to sleep. He did the same at Mass as a way of keeping them still. The boys understood, in a way that children shouldn't, how precious every second could be, and no one wanted to miss a chance to hold a hand, wrap their arms around each other, or give a kiss.

When Joe loves, he loves hard; he's all in. He was always holding my hand, putting his arm around me, or brushing the hair from my face. I realized that physical affection played an important role in his entire family. Val couldn't walk by the boys without reaching out to touch their shoulders or brush their heads. Their parents stopped by often to shower the boys with kisses. The whole lot of them were huggers.

Being thrust into this group was a strange and uncomfortable development for me. I wasn't used to public shows of affection. Like my mom, I was unwilling—and maybe even unable—to be openly emotional. My family wasn't cold—they were incredibly loving—but outside of a long good-bye, kissing and hugging just wasn't a part of our routine, with Grandmom Jacobs as the one exception. In truth, I'm a bit of an introvert, and I sometimes found all that affection draining. Joe can do a rally with thousands of people and leave feeling energized and ready to take on the world. He connects with people so easily, and he never hesitates when a stranger wants to tell him something personal or give him a hug. But I have always had a difficult time keeping up with his energy, and I need more space and quiet time to recover after any kind of public or social event.

Still, I began to realize that our relationship wasn't just a shift to my life—it was a shift for the Bidens as well.

It was around 9:00 in the morning when I heard the front door of Joe's house open. He had left for Washington on the 7:30 train, and Beau and Hunt had gone to school. My mind quickly scanned through the people who might possibly turn up. *Oh no.*

Standing with my hands in a sink basin full of dirty dishes, my stomach dropped. There was only one person I could think of who might come by, and it was the worst person to see me standing here in her son's kitchen at 9:00 a.m. when no one else was home. I imagined escape routes or perhaps hiding in the broom closet as the footsteps moved down the hall. But there was no time. As I'd feared, Joe's mother strode into the kitchen and stopped short with a look of surprise.

For the briefest of moments, I considered telling her I'd just dropped by, that I was surprising Joe with clean dishes . . . ten hours before he would be home. But I knew better than to lie to Mom Mom.

Jean Finnegan Biden—or *Mom Mom,* as everybody called her—was a small, white-haired powerhouse of a woman. She was the essence of the Irish-Catholic matriarch, outspoken in her opinions and unflinchingly loyal to her children and grandchildren. I had heard stories of her maternal ferocity, including a time when she'd humiliated a nun—one of Joe's teachers—who had mocked Joe's stutter in front of his class. No matter his age, she adored her "Joey" and would do anything to protect him and the boys, especially after all that had happened. And now, she'd stumbled upon me standing in her son's kitchen in the early-morning hours.

"Ah, Jill. I've been wanting to talk to you," she said with a level stare.

I braced myself for a lecture, or maybe a warning against toying with the people she loved. Whatever she had to say, I knew it wouldn't be easy to hear.

"I don't know where this is going between you and Joe, but I want to thank you."

I was stunned. "For what?" I asked.

"For making my son believe he could love again," she said. It was the last thing I expected to hear—and it left me dumbfounded as to how I could respond to such a kindness.

Mom Mom was understandably wary of me, a twenty-four-year-old suddenly entering her family's life just as they were beginning to get back to some kind of normal. Honestly, as a mother of grown children now, I would be every bit as cautious as she was. There's always a part of you that wants to step into your children's lives and make the right decisions for them— pick them up when they stray and put them on the safest, easiest path, just as we did when they were small. But the tragedy of being a good parent is that the better you are at your job, the less you will be allowed to swoop in and protect the people you love most in the world. You have no choice but to trust that they'll do their best and hope that fate will be kind. She could see that her son was happy again. And in the end, that was what mattered.

Which is not to say she was relinquishing her matriarchal power. After Joe and I were married, she was always happy to tell me how to take care of the boys. "I heard Hunter isn't feeling well," she'd say. "Did you call Dr. Borin?"

"No, not yet," I'd reply.

"Well, call him right now," she'd say, "and I'll call you back in ten minutes to hear what he said."

Still, from that moment in the kitchen on, I understood the depth of her love for Joe. And because of that, she opened up her heart to me. She was a strong woman, and one who would go on to become my role model on mothering and grandmothering in many ways. I learned more from her than I would have ever guessed standing there embarrassed and half-dressed in her son's kitchen.

In her final years, Mom Mom lived in a little house at the top of our driveway—a guesthouse Joe and I had prepared for her, knowing she'd be more comfortable living close by. Every night before going to bed, Joe would walk up to the top of the drive to check in on her. They had a nightly ritual of eating a bowl of ice cream together, just the two of them, and she always made sure she had his favorite: chocolate chip. I used to tease Joe when he'd come back down the hill with the smell of ice cream on his breath like a kid getting away with something. But I secretly loved that they had this time together.

As my kids have grown up, we have less and less time alone—it's the natural progression of family. Mothers come second to wives and husbands and children, as they should. I understand that, but like most mothers, there's a part of me that mourns it, too. So I loved that, after all those years of raising a family and launching a career and juggling all the other important pieces of adulthood, Mom Mom got to have those moments back at the end—just her and Joey. That was really special, and I'm grateful we had her so close, for so long.

As nervous as I'd been about meeting Joe's family, I was almost as nervous about introducing him to mine. He was the first serious relationship I'd had since my divorce, and it was important that my family like him and the boys.

We'd been dating for about four months when my parents had their twenty-fifth wedding anniversary. Grandmom and Grandpop planned a party in their backyard, with lunch and a sheet cake on a picnic table, and I decided I might as well get it over with and bring Joe and the boys to Hammonton. In one overwhelming day, they could meet the whole family at once.

I was anxious about the meeting and wanted to have a little time with everyone first, so I asked Joe to drop me off at Grandmom and Grandpop's, and come back an hour later. He took Beau and Hunt to a pizza place a few blocks away.

Everyone was at the house when I arrived, and when I told them Joe and the boys were coming in about an hour, Grandmom's face lit up. She was a lifelong Democrat, so she was absolutely thrilled that I was dating Joe. Everyone was excited to meet him, but she was glowing.

Joe drove up the sand-gravel driveway next to Grandmom's house, and as soon as she saw his car, she bolted out of the kitchen and down the porch steps. And then, as if she'd known him her entire life, my little grandmother, in her housecoat and apron, strode right up to Joe with her arms wide. "Oh, honey," she said. "It's so good to see you!" He bent down to hug her, and she proudly exclaimed, "I'm a Democrat, too, you know! I worked for President Roosevelt on the WPA." Joe laughed, and my grandmother took his hand and led him into the backyard, with the boys following behind.

My grandparents had a garden with long rows of tomato plants along one wall, a tiny piece of Italy right there in New Jersey, and just as Joe was walking past them, two little girls popped out—my twin sisters, who were then eight years old. Grandpop came up behind, chasing them with tomato-leaf fangs and roaring like a monster. He dropped his disguise, and then he, too, greeted Joe with an enormous hug, as if he were family who had been away rather than the complete and total stranger he was.

Joe fit right in and immediately had everyone laughing, so he was easy for them to love. And like Grandmom, the Jacobses may have been a little impressed that a senator was gracing their backyard cookout. But mostly, my family could tell I was finding joy in this new relationship.

Joe told me years later that this was the moment he felt he could win me. My family seemed to adore him, and he was sure they'd be on his side when he asked me to marry him. Even if I was confused at the time about what I wanted, he could see how important family was to me, and he knew I would want it again, eventually. He was surer every day that I was the missing piece in the Biden puzzle. But it would be a long time—and many proposals—before I would agree.

6

FIVE PROPOSALS

The first time Joe proposed, he simply said, "I want us to get married." It wasn't a big deal—just an ordinary conversation on an ordinary day. I already knew how he felt, so it didn't come as a surprise. I also knew I couldn't say yes. But unbeknownst to me, Joe wasn't just asking on his own accord. Beau and Hunter had recently cornered him in the bathroom one morning while he was shaving. "Beau thinks we should get married," six-year-old Hunter told him. With their father understandably confused by this pronouncement, seven-year-old Beau explained, "We think we should marry Jill."

Hearing that story later, I had to laugh—how often do our children understand the obvious answer before we do?

In the months prior to that conversation, the boys and I had been spending a lot of time together. When Joe worked late, I would go over to make dinner and keep them company. I would help pick them up from school sometimes, or we'd pass an evening watching TV. We started to build our own relationship separate from their dad.

Even at a young age, Beau was a lot like Joe. He was incredibly articulate and would never hesitate to express how he was feeling. He was kind and responsible.

Hunt was more like me. He didn't want to talk about his feelings as much, and he didn't always know how to express them when he was a kid, but he would always show you with his actions—he was warm and loving. If we were waiting in a lobby or watching TV, he would throw his arms around my neck and rest his head on my shoulder. He would look up at me with a twinkle of adventure in his eyes, and I knew we were going to have fun.

I was surprised by how much I enjoyed getting to know them, and though I had been a little hesitant about dating someone with kids, I found myself excited when I got to see them. I realized during those months how happy I was spending time with the boys. But that didn't mean I was ready to get married.

I saw my mother cry only one time, at my dad's funeral. She didn't even cry when her own parents died. I saw that stoicism as strength—and that strength was what I wanted for myself more than anything. I decided early that I would never let my emotions rule me.

I worked hard to live up to that with the kids, always fighting to keep control of myself, especially in times of hardship and adversity. They never saw me cry when Joe was lying near death at Walter Reed hospital after his two aneurysms in 1988, or when EMTs carried him down the steps of our house on a stretcher after he had a pulmonary embolism that same year. I shed no tears in front of them when we pulled out of the

2008 presidential race after a disappointing finish in Iowa, even though inside I was crushed.

As a political spouse, I've found that my stoicism often serves me well. In 1988, when Joe's first presidential campaign started to look bleak, people were constantly looking for cracks in our team. We all felt scrutinized, but I refused to show weakness. And later, when Beau got sick, we didn't want it to become a national conversation—it was just too personal. We were holding out hope that he would recover. So we kept it to ourselves, and with the exception of a select few people, no one knew. I continued teaching, continued attending events. I lived a double life, smiling publicly but worrying constantly on the inside about my son. To say it was difficult would be an understatement. But I also knew I couldn't just put aside my jobs of Second Lady and college professor. I compartmentalized the pain, and my stoicism helped me keep going.

In many ways, Joe's temperament and mine complement each other. He tends to pull me out of my shell, and I help keep him grounded. He's affectionate enough for both of us. Even now, his staff members laugh about it, joking that the answer to "Where's the vice president?" is always, "Well, where is *she?*"

After the disappointment of my divorce, I never wanted to feel so out of control of my heart again. But in the months that Joe and I were dating, that desire ran up against a new reality: I was falling in love.

Still, marriage meant something different to me by that point. I knew that it was harder to unite two lives than I had imagined growing up. I knew that relationships could be fragile. I knew that, no matter how much I tried, there would be so much that I couldn't control. If I gave Joe my whole heart, he had the power to break it. What if he changed his mind? What if it didn't work? What if I took another chance, and I was left humiliated? What if I failed?

There were times when I actually prayed *not* to get married. "Please," I would beg God, "don't let me make that mistake again."

"Jill," Joe said to me a few months after his first proposal, "I love you. I want to get married. I want the boys to have a mother, to make our family complete." But I didn't feel any closer to saying yes than I had the first time he asked.

I was slowly learning to trust again, because Joe and the boys made me feel secure in their love. But even as my fears of getting my heart broken began to lessen, other fears took their place. Being Joe's wife would mean a life in the spotlight that I had never wanted. I was a college student when we'd first met, and I liked living under the radar. Joe lived with constant public visibility.

But it was more than just the pressures of public life. I had always wanted my own career—and a year after we started dating, I finally landed a job I loved, teaching ninth- and tenth-grade English at a private Catholic high school in Wilmington called Saint Mark's. My students were smart and respectful, and I loved hearing them come alive in the classroom during spirited discussions of Shakespeare, Dickens, and Thoreau. Because I looked so young—I wasn't much older than the upperclassmen, after all—I wore my long hair up in a bun and attempted to carry myself with some gravitas. Even so, I had to laugh when I heard some of the kids whispering, "Did you hear? Miss Jacobs is dating *Senator Biden!*" After a student saw Joe and me together at a gas station, the news had spread like a firestorm through the school.

I was launching my career and planning for graduate school—and then I had staff calling to schedule dates with my boyfriend around his insane Senate schedule. I was being pulled in so many directions. I knew that if I married Joe, I'd have to give up my apartment, the only space that was just for me. I'd have to quit my job for the boys' sake, to give them the time to acclimate to having someone new in the house every day and not just on weekends. And I'd have to become Jill Biden, senator's wife. It was all too much.

After attending events and dinners with Joe, I'd come home and throw myself on my bed in my sparse apartment. Exhausted, I'd stare at the divots in the ceiling and mentally check through all the things I had to do. When I finally stopped my mind from racing, only one thought was left: *What am I doing?*

Joe kept trying, asking me a third time, then a few months later, a fourth. My answer was still "not yet"—but over almost two years of being together, the reason had shifted again.

At this point, I was no longer afraid of marriage; I knew I could marry Joe. He was a good man and a caring partner, and I was unquestionably in love with him. He would make a great husband. And in the unlikely event that something went wrong down the road, I knew I could survive. As time moved me further and further from the pain of my earlier relationship, I realized that, as bad as it felt, I had survived. I was resilient.

It was also no longer about my job or having my space. I was happy spending most of my time with him and the boys. And I could see Joe would support my desire to have a career—he was always encouraging as I studied to get my master's degree, and we had talked about the fact that teaching was a part of who I was. He even came to a student production of *King Lear* to support me in my studies. It was done in Kabuki style and was absolutely unbearable, but he sat through the entire thing. We laughed the whole way home.

At this point, I knew that marrying Joe wasn't just about him. It was about Hunter and Beau as well. They had endured the loss of one mother already, and I couldn't risk having them lose another.

Joe often drove the boys to school. It was a big part of their day—getting special alone time with their dad every morning. Their shared ritual was to sing along to songs on the radio, and one of their favorites was the Helen Reddy hit "You and Me Against the World." It's a simple, beautiful song in which a mother sings to her child that she'll always be there for her: *When all the others turn their backs and walk away / You can count on me to stay.*

That was their bond: one of shared memories, of grief, of absolute trust. It was them against the world. And they were asking me to join that sacred circle. They trusted me to step into their lives and give them the love and devotion that had been stolen from them. They weren't afraid that I wouldn't measure up. But I was. After all they had been through, I could never risk hurting them again. I had to be 100 percent sure that if Joe and I got married, it would be forever—for Beau and Hunter's sake.

By then, we were acting more like a family than two people

dating. We were a foursome, and we did everything together. When Thanksgiving rolled around, we knew we wanted to spend it together, but we didn't know where. My parents wanted us to join them, his parents wanted us to join them, and even Neilia's parents had extended an invitation. We were touched and grateful, but it was stressful to think about choosing one family gathering over another, so I said to Joe, "Let's go somewhere, just the four of us."

Joe's chief of staff, Wes Barthelmes, suggested Nantucket, and although neither Joe nor I had ever been, we decided that sounded as good as anywhere. I packed a cooler with sandwiches and sodas, we loaded the boys into a station wagon, and we drove six hours to the Cape. On a packed ferryboat to the island, we chugged past beautiful Brant Point Lighthouse and up to the pier. Joe and I took deep breaths of salt-tinged air as we got our first view of the shingled cottages that lined the coast. It was like sailing into an Edward Hopper painting—the cool blues and greens, the sun bouncing off white lighthouses. That first year, we stayed in one of those cottages, right on the water, paying one hundred dollars for the whole week.

Nantucket Thanksgiving became our tradition for the next four decades. With a few exceptions, we've made the trek every year since, creating rituals that would become a key part of our family along the way. We always pack sandwiches and eat them on the road. We toss a few catalogs in the back seat and tell the kids—first Beau and Hunter, then Ashley, and now our grandkids—to circle what they want for Christmas. We always took the ferry, which the boys loved as kids—that is, until we began using Air Force Two in the White House. Once in Nantucket, we spend hours poking around in the shops, and on the Friday after Thanksgiving, we go to the Brotherhood of Thieves restaurant for lunch. We gather on cobblestoned Main Street on Friday evening to see Santa Claus, watch the big Christmas tree–lighting ceremony, and sing carols. And for many years, we posed for a family photo in front of a charming seaside cottage with a sign in front that read: FOREVER WILD.

Nantucket, dinners together, Christmas photos, and new traditions big and small—day by day, we were becoming a unit, whether I had agreed to marriage or not. Over the years, I've been asked what decisions helped form our family. But they were so rarely made overtly—our lives just began to follow a natural rhythm. We didn't speak of it, but there was a driving force behind it all: We were becoming whole again—Joe and the boys, and me as well. I was in love with all of them. They were putting their faith in me, and I had to live up to it.

One afternoon in the spring of 1977, Joe stopped by my apartment on his way to the airport. He was heading out on a congressional delegation to South Africa, which meant we wouldn't see each other for the next ten days—our longest time apart since we'd started dating. I hugged him and told him to be safe, but something felt different. As he was walking out the door, he turned back to me.

"Look," he said. "I've been as patient as I know how to be, but this has got my Irish up. Either you decide to marry me, or that's it—I'm out. I'm not asking again." His blue eyes, normally alight, seemed clouded with gray. "I'm too much in love with you to just be friends."

I had known this moment would come. He'd first proposed

almost two years before. Of course he wouldn't wait forever. We stood for a moment looking at each other, and I nodded.

"When I come back," he said, "I need an answer, yes or no. You don't have to tell me *when*. You just have to tell me *if*."

"Okay," I told him. And then he was gone.

Over the next few days, I thought about my life—what it had been so far, and what it could be. I loved Joe. I adored the boys. I couldn't bear the thought of losing them. When Joe told me this was the last time he would ask, I was sure he meant it. He was prepared to walk away forever.

Saying yes meant changing the trajectory of my entire life at age twenty-five. On the other hand, saying no meant walking away from three people I had grown to love more than anyone. But I was still afraid of what could go wrong—for me, for Joe, for the boys.

C. S. Lewis wrote *The Four Loves* about the different needs we all have in our relationships, the bonds that make up our lives, and how they are reflective of our connection to God. In it, he writes at length about the dilemma I faced:

> To love at all is to be vulnerable. Love anything, and your heart will be wrung and possibly broken. If you want to make sure of keeping it intact, you must give your heart to no one, not even to an animal. Wrap it carefully round with hobbies and little luxuries; avoid all entanglements; lock it up safe in the casket or coffin of your selfishness. But in that casket—safe, dark, motionless, airless—it will change. It will not be broken; it will become unbreakable, impenetrable, irredeemable. The

alternative to tragedy, or at least to the risk of tragedy, is damnation. The only place outside Heaven where you can be perfectly safe from all the dangers and perturbations of love is Hell.

The evening Joe got back from South Africa, he didn't drive home from the airport but came straight to my apartment. I was expecting him to pick me up so we could go to a big family dinner at his house—with Mom Mom, Dada, Val and Jack, Frank, and the boys—but he didn't seem to be in much of a party mood when I opened the door. I invited him in, but even after the long flight, he had no intention of relaxing for a moment. He stood firm in my foyer and fixed his eyes on me. "I want to know your answer," he said.

I could see that he didn't want to lose me, but he would walk away for his boys. There was concern in the corners of his eyes, a sternness, and I wondered if the fears that were still nagging at the back of my mind were as visible. But even in the tension of that small entryway, I could feel his love, and I knew it was forever, unconditional. I knew that he and the boys had my heart, and we were too interwined now to protect ourselves from each other. Marriage license or not, we were already a family.

I looked at him and quietly said, "Yes."

Relief flooded his face as he wrapped me in a hug. Then he held my shoulders and looked me straight in the eye. "I promise you, your life will never change," he said.

That night at dinner, we kept it a secret from the rest of the family, though I wonder if they knew something was different. Across the table, I could see the tension in his posture was gone—he laughed a little louder and looked at me with a grateful affection. And as I settled into the thought of our marriage, my doubts dissipated. I looked around the table at my family and knew I had made the right choice.

In the years since, I've thought about Joe's promise that night, that life would "never change." It would turn out to be wildly untrue, of course. Life is change. And our lives would be more amazing and more unbearably difficult than we could have known as we smiled at each other over dinner that night. There have been tragedies. We have had our hearts wrung and broken. But the only place we are safe from all the dangers of love is hell. And one thing in my life *has* stayed the same: Joe and I have always had each other.

A year ago, for Christmas, he wrote me a book of poems. My favorite goes:

> I had lost all hope for the future
> But the moment I saw you I knew
> I worked so hard to get you to say I do
> When you did—you made the world anew

He promised me love, and through losses and victories, through births and deaths, through the evolution of our family, that has never changed.

On June 17, 1977, wearing a white eyelet dress, I took my place next to Joe at the altar of the U.N. Chapel in midtown Manhattan. As the priest started the marriage ceremony, Beau and Hunter stood up suddenly from the red velvet pews and made their way to the altar. They took their place beside Joe without saying a word. The boys hadn't discussed it, and they didn't ask anyone; they just instinctively understood that this was a marriage of the four of us. These precious little boys knew the obvious better than anyone else: that for richer or poorer, in sickness and health, it was us against the world.

7

WE DON'T SAY "STEP"

Jill, aren't you ever going to wash our clothes?" asked a slightly exasperated eight-year-old Beau, holding a pair of dirty socks.

After Joe and I married, I felt like I needed time at home with the boys to figure out our new normal. Joe and Val, with the support of the entire Biden family, had done an incredible job creating a home where Hunt and Beau felt safe and loved. But even so, the boys had already had to adapt to too much upheaval, and this change—even though it was one they wanted—required yet another adjustment. I wanted to build on the foundation that was already there and make sure they felt as secure with me as I had with my family. Like Val and Mom Mom, I knew I couldn't replace Mommy—as the boys would always call Neilia—but I could give them back some of what they had lost. So I left my teaching job behind for the time being to stay home full-time with Hunter and Beau.

Like most new parents, I had very little idea what I was doing.

Growing up the oldest of five girls, I had spent my share

of time playing parent. I looked out for my sisters, mediated fights, and helped out around the house. But as a single adult, I had grown used to living on my own and keeping up a tiny apartment. I also had no experience with boys. And Beau and Hunt truly were sweaty, messy *boys*.

One afternoon, I was upstairs in our bedroom when I heard Beau and Hunt bang through the front door into the house. "Come look! Hurry!" they yelled, and I rushed downstairs to see what the fuss was about. Beau was holding a net, his face lit up with excitement. "Look what we found!" Hunter beamed. I bent down and there, coiled in the net, was a snake. I screamed and ran back upstairs, slamming the bedroom door shut behind me. The boys called Joe in D.C. to tell him they had scared me into hiding. In all my imaginings of what it would be like to have boys, I did not think there would be literal "snakes and snails."

They played every kind of sport, regularly skinning their knees or spraining ankles. They were rambunctious and loud. They tore holes in all their jeans and came home covered in mud. Which is why it shouldn't have come as a surprise when always-helpful Beau pulled me aside that day in the kitchen.

"What do you mean, 'aren't I ever going to wash your clothes?'" I asked. "I do it every week."

"You should probably do it every day," he said, attempting in his eight-year-old way to be tactful. Yes, this was going to be an adjustment. But I soon realized Beau had a point—there was no other way to keep up with two boys who got themselves into every mess imaginable.

So, for the next two years, I did the laundry daily. I bandaged cut elbows and nursed away fevers. I picked the boys up from

Wilmington Friends School in the afternoon. I took them to their soccer games and their Catholic catechism classes and made sure dinner was on the table every night. I went to school with the other moms on Hot Dog Day, when we'd cook hot dogs in the school's tiny kitchen, load them into a cart, and then roll it down the hallway, delivering lunch to all the kids in their classrooms. And I volunteered at the school library, checking out and shelving books. Whenever I was there, the boys would bring their friends by to say hi. I could tell they were showing me off—their new "mom."

It was not lost on me that I was living a love story intended for someone else. My parents had built their lives together from the beginning, but I had inherited a family that another woman had started. I had no guidance on how to navigate marrying a widower. Even *The Brady Bunch,* a show focused entirely on the blending of a family not unlike mine, never explicitly mentioned the spouses who came before Carol and Mike.

After we got married, Joe and I took the boys to upstate New York to visit Neilia's family, the Hunters. Neilia grew up in a gorgeous little lake town called Skaneateles, and though her parents had moved to Florida, they still spent their summers there. I can't imagine what they thought when they first met me—Joe's new bride, around the same age as Neilia had been when they last saw her. They must have seen the future they'd imagined for their daughter now stretching out before someone else. They could have felt resentful of the woman who'd married their son-in-law, or become hardened toward me by grief. But they welcomed me into their home with hugs instead.

In the summers, Joe and I would drive Beau and Hunter up to their lake house so the boys could spend a couple of weeks with their grandparents. We sent them down to Florida for Easter break, and Dada and Mom Mom Hunter would take them to Disney World. They were a part of our family.

And Neilia's memory lived on outside of our family as well.

One of the first political events I attended was a picnic kicking off Joe's 1978 Senate campaign. This was a huge event held at Joe's alma mater, Archmere Academy, with hundreds of volunteers and supporters. It marked the first time I would be introduced to the people of Delaware and the Democratic Party as Joe's wife.

We had never made any official announcement of our engagement, and I hadn't told anyone beforehand of our intention to get married except immediate family. A wedding in either Wilmington or D.C. would most likely draw the press, and we wanted to keep it small and intimate—which is why we decided to marry in the U.N. Chapel in New York. When it was time to apply for our marriage certificate, we took the train up and caught a taxi to the city clerk's office in the Bronx. There, we joined a long line of families with little girls in crinoline slips and bakery boxes with small wedding cakes. Joe and I filled out the paperwork, then sat and waited for the clerk to type everything up. To my relief, no one seemed to be taking any notice of us. After about fifteen minutes, we heard a loud voice calling, "Bidden! . . . *BIDDEN!*" I burst out laughing, turning to Joe. "Well, it looks like our secret is still safe!"

But now, I was officially Mrs. Biden, and that came with a public requirement. We'd been so private in our two years together that nobody outside our friends and family knew very much about me. At our first public outing, a picnic, people actually started lining up to say hello and shake my hand. "It's so nice to meet you!" they'd exclaim, or they'd offer earnest congratulations on the wedding. Soon, people began saying things like, "I knew Neilia," and telling me stories about her. Some even took me by the shoulders, saying, "Let me get a look at you." These women were longtime Democratic supporters who'd taken Joe under their wing, and I knew they meant well. People were personally invested in Joe's life, especially after the accident. So many prayers had gone up for his family—prayers like my own. So many hearts had grieved for his loss. And now it was time for the protective constituents of Delaware to size me up against what they thought Joe deserved. No one was unkind, though the scrutiny was overwhelming. Still, I knew I had to get through it for his sake, so I stood there and smiled and shook every last hand.

When the picnic was finally over, Joe pulled me into a hug. "Honey, I'm sorry," he said. "They weren't thinking." I told him I understood—and I did. But when we got home after the picnic, I went straight up to the bedroom and closed the door. I just needed to sit by myself for a while, to collect my thoughts.

It's hard to know what you owe a spouse who died before you came along. A lot of people wrestle with the fact that the love of their lives loved someone else first—and perhaps never stopped loving that person. Some people feel jealousy. Some people feel inadequate. Some people let questions of what would have been eat away at their peace of mind. As President Theodore Roosevelt is rumored to have said, "Comparison is the thief of joy."

I understand those complicated emotions, but I have never felt threatened by Neilia. Joe has always made sure that I feel his love for me—in fact, he often jokes that he loves me more than I love him. How can he measure that? I don't know, but from the beginning, I knew that if he could love Neilia that deeply, that completely, then maybe I could be loved that completely, too. And that this could be the love I had long been looking for—the kind of love my parents had.

Joe used to tell the boys that "Mommy sent Jill to us." He believed it, so the boys did as well. How else could they make any sense of the injustice of losing their mother and sister? They had to have faith that the incredible love Neilia had for them could keep going—could somehow bring them a person who would love them as much as they needed. The boys clung to that faith as they grew up. It was a gift Joe gave them—a way to make sense of the world.

I didn't want Neilia's memory hidden away. I didn't want the boys to think they had to choose between us or feel like they had to put aside that part of themselves. And so we made space for her. We didn't live in the home Neilia had shared with Joe, but she was there, nonetheless. We kept her pictures displayed around the house. She reappeared in Joe's stories. I knew the boys carried a piece of her with them, and I caught glimpses of what I knew must be her laugh, the crinkle of her nose, the curve of her brow in their faces. I wanted Joe to remind them over and over again just how much she loved them. Because she would always be their mother. There was no "us" without her.

Every December 18, the day of the accident, we made the world stop. Joe stayed home from work, and the boys went in late to school. We went together to the 7:00 a.m. Mass at our parish, St. Joseph's Catholic Church in Wilmington. After that, Joe and the boys would go to the cemetery, while I went home and prepared coffee, bagels, fruit salad, and yogurt for the extended family—Jack and Val, Mom Mom and Dada, and whoever else wanted to come by. Joe had told me that Neilia loved white roses, so I would buy a grave blanket and add three white roses with baby's breath—one for Joe, Hunter, and Beau. I put it in the back of Joe's car so he didn't have to think about it. When they got to the cemetery, he and the boys could share their moments and memories together.

For years, I never joined them; it was their time with Neilia. But the year after Beau died, for the first time, I went with Joe. I held his hand as we stood there in the chilly December morning, and I thought of the words I knew were spoken at her eulogy: "Death lies on her like an untimely frost / Upon the sweetest flower of all the field." I thought about the family we had made together—the three of us. I owed her so much: my loyalty, my gratitude for the gift of these beautiful boys, and yes, my love. And if, indeed, she had sent me, I hope she's grateful she did.

As the weeks passed, the boys and I began to settle into a routine. Every night, I'd make a hot meal, and the three of us would eat it together since Joe wouldn't get home until 7:30 or 8:00 p.m. Like my mother always had, I tried to make our dinners feel special with a prepared table and lit candles. Dinner became a tradition and hub for our new family, just as it had been for mine, and it was a constant the boys could depend upon.

When Joe got home, it was time for dessert together before

bed—his special time with the kids. He almost never missed bedtime, even when he was exhausted after getting off the train "smelling like work," as Ashley would say years later. He would scratch their backs and tell them stories as they fell asleep. That's a task that still falls to him today when our grand-kids stay over. Beau's children, little Hunter and Natalie, love to hear stories about when Beau was a little boy, just like Hunter's daughters, Naomi, Finnegan, and Maisy, liked hearing stories about their dad when they were younger. Joe, the family racon-teur, is the only one who can tell them perfectly.

Even beyond our nightly dinner and dessert routines before bedtime, food took on special meaning in our young family, as it had in Joe's family and mine growing up. The boys' birthdays were just a year and a day apart, on February 3 and February 4, so we'd make each one's favorite meal and dessert on alternat-ing years. One year, Beau got to choose, and we'd have every-one over for a feast of pasta and brownies. The next year would be Hunter's choice, and we'd have his favorites, my homemade chicken potpie and ice cream. Birthdays became annual family parties, with extended relatives coming to the house for the big meal, cake, balloons, and piles of presents. Mom Mom never seemed to have any wrapping paper and would always wrap her presents for the boys in newspaper. I'd have Post-it notes all over the house, with everything we needed to do for the parties. It was a lot of work, but we wanted to make the boys feel like they were the most important people in the world.

And there were more traditions to come. On Christmas Eve, we'd have a big dinner of pasta at our house, and then the boys would wait for the firefighters to visit. Every year, the local fire company would decorate a truck with cartoon characters, then drive it slowly through the neighborhoods, blowing the siren and tossing candy to people who came out to wave. They always made a quick stop at our house, and I made sure we had eggnog and Christmas cookies for them. The boys loved it, the visit adding a touch of celebrity to an already magical night.

We started a Secret Santa among all the cousins—Jimmy's kids, Frank's kids, Val's kids, and Beau and Hunt. Val and I would pick names out of a hat, but we always rigged it a little bit so Val could give gifts to Beau and Hunter and I could give one to her daughter, Missy. After a couple of years, the kids caught on, and they'd joke about how the Secret Santa drawing always just happened to turn out the same way.

And it was Christmas when the boys gave me Neilia's engagement ring. Joe had initially planned to melt it down and make two rings, one for each boy to give his eventual bride. But it was a beautiful ring that represented too much to be split in two, so instead, the boys decided I should wear it.

I didn't have the words to tell them how much it meant to me. I gave them each a hug and said, "I'm honored to wear this ring. But it will always belong to you." We decided it would be passed on to the first granddaughter in our family.

Twenty years later, Hunter's daughter Naomi was born— named, of course, after baby Naomi. It's particularly fitting that one day the ring will be hers, and I hope she passes it on to her children as well, keeping the tradition, and the memory of Neilia, alive.

It's funny the way that small things take on meaning—like how the *pop* and *crack* of a vinyl record become an integral part of the old songs we love. The spontaneous choice to throw a catalog in the back seat for the road trip; the concession of one more treat before bed; a last-minute decision to invite everyone to birthday dinner—these become sacred rituals we return to again and again. The simple act of cooking a hot dog or drawing a name out of a hat is a renewal of our vows to each other: I love you. I choose you. No matter what happens, you can count on this. You can count on *me*.

One morning, I was in the bedroom when Joe sent the boys in to give me a kiss good-bye before catching the bus. As Hunter and Beau hugged and kissed me, they said, "Love you, Mom." It was without thought, so casual—as mundane as the particulars of crustless sandwiches and dirty socks. There was never a discussion, never a reckoning about what it meant for me to go from *Jill* to *Mom*. They loved me. And I loved them, more than I dreamed I would.

When *People* magazine did a story about us shortly after we were married, the reporter asked Beau about his "stepmom." Beau was adamant: "We don't have a stepmom." In confusion, the editor called Joe's press secretary. The magazine had found reports on Neilia and Naomi, so they were confused: Hadn't the boys' mother died? What did Beau mean? Joe's press secretary just laughed and explained that the boys insisted on calling me their mom, not their stepmom. Beau and Hunt never relented in this point; over the years, they would proudly correct well-meaning friends and reporters who felt a need to define our relationship on their terms: "We don't say 'step.'"

Before they could even put the feeling into words, the boys had understood intrinsically that sometimes, when people said *step*, what they meant was "not real." This isn't always the case, of course; I know a lot of families that embrace the many terms describing their unique relationships: *stepmom, bonus parent, half-sibling*. But *stepmom* just wasn't right for us—or more accurately, for the boys. It was important to me that Beau and Hunter felt our family was whole, and that meant we got to define our relationship, not anyone else.

The fact that some people pushed back on that was frustrating for all of us. One year, when a cable television host interviewed Joe and me on his talk show, he referred to Beau and Hunter as my stepchildren. I gently corrected him, saying, "We don't say 'step,'" but he wouldn't let it go, insisting that "technically" the boys were my stepsons. Intended or not, when people displayed their unwillingness to let us set the terms of our own family, it felt like a judgment, a dividing line between what they counted as true family versus mere proximity.

Whether it's adoption, divorce, same-sex marriage, or any number of iterations of family, the simple truth is that people should be able to define their own relationships. And so that's what we've done. In our family, Neilia would always be Mommy, but I was Mom. There was room enough, there was love enough, for us all.

8

THIS IS YOUR BABY

Some people seem to believe that a parent—usually the mother—will not, or even *cannot* love a nonbiological child the same way she loves her biological child. Many believe that DNA alone can cement the bonds between a child and a parent, an opinion people were even more vocal about in the time when Beau and Hunter were little. And I've found this worry over maternal connection isn't limited to the realm of blending families—in a world overflowing with parenting advice, we've been told that everything from C-sections to formula to day care can result in degrees of detachment from our kids.

I knew I loved the boys more and more with each day that passed. But there was a part of me that wondered: Would I love them the same if I had given birth to them? I couldn't imagine feeling more strongly than I already did—and I hoped I would give all of my children the same amount of care, discipline, and attention. Isn't that what a good parent did? And yet, I had never had a biological child. I couldn't know for sure.

When Joe and I were first married, I told him that our family was perfect just the way it was. We had two amazing boys, and

I didn't want any more kids. It was true. I had my hands full with them and with my mission to integrate myself into their lives. In short time, our little foursome had fallen into a natural rhythm—Joe establishing himself more and more as a leader in the Senate, the boys excelling in school and sports, and me growing in my role as a mom. I learned to embrace, both literally and figuratively, my boys, who loved to cuddle, curling up with them in the evenings to watch *Happy Days* on the love seat. I went to every single game they had—a seemingly endless schedule of soccer, football, tennis, baseball, and basketball—and always cheered the loudest. I became comfortable with the less ideal parts of motherhood, like disciplining them. I was no longer afraid that getting frustrated at the boys over a ruined sweater or sending them to their room over trouble at school would break our relationship. Because that's what parents do.

It wasn't just a title; I was their mom in every sense of the word. They knew it, and I knew it. And ever since the day they had first called me *Mom* in passing, I realized that we had done it. We had built that safe home I'd always wanted.

From that time on, I had no more anxiety that we might let them down. The boys were happy; they were thriving. We were a unit, strong and secure. And a funny thing happened: all that love made me want more. It was as if the fear I had been holding on to—that I wasn't enough—had disappeared, and in its place was something else: space in our hearts to keep growing, a new chair at the table waiting to be filled.

I distinctly remember the disgust I felt when I found out my mother was pregnant. I was fifteen, and though there was a part of me that understood she had had sex with my father at some point—long ago, and only in order to conceive me, Jan, and Bonny—I had no idea that they were *still* doing it. It was a time when squeamish sitcoms refused to acknowledge even the existence of toilets, and there was no internet or sex ed to educate us, so teenagers like me had to turn to *Valley of the Dolls* to develop our limited understanding of the mysteries of the bedroom. My mother was thirty-five, far too ancient an age, I was sure, to engage in such activities. But I had the proof, in all its shame, in my indignant hands.

I'd been looking through her drawer for something and found a card one of my aunts had sent, saying, "Congratulations on your new baby!" Stunned, I confronted her, waving the note in her face like a spouse betrayed. "I found this in your drawer," I sneered. "Are you pregnant?!"

She was.

"Mom!" I cried. "*How* could you sleep with Daddy? You're not *still* doing it, are you?" She said nothing, just slyly smiled. "You have to promise me you will *never, ever* sleep with him again," I begged. And so, she promised, though she obviously had no intention of keeping it.

My mother grew huge during her pregnancy, and she wore the same outfit day in and day out—or at least that's how I see her in my mind. I can picture her so clearly, standing in the kitchen, dressed in what might as well be a tent, with the veins in her legs blue and swollen. She seemed enormous, and I was mortified by her. I tried to steer my friends away from her at the house, or better yet, keep them from coming over at all so they wouldn't see her. I couldn't wait for it to be over, even though it meant we'd have a crying baby in the house—another prospect I didn't like one bit.

And then, to the shock of us all, she had not one crying baby but two. Twins! Bonny and Jan were ecstatic, but I was just annoyed.

As this was my most lasting association with pregnancy, it was not something I'd ever looked forward to. There were so many reasons not to have a baby—but as time went on, they seemed less and less important. I felt a growing desire to fill that space that had opened up. I didn't tell Joe for several months, but eventually, I couldn't keep it to myself.

We were having a date night in Philadelphia and had gone into the Bellevue-Stratford Hotel bar for a drink. "I know that I'd said I was fine with two children," I told Joe. "But I want to have another." Joe's eyes widened with surprise—we had always agreed that two children were enough for our family. He didn't say no, and he didn't say yes. It was a big decision, and I knew he had to think about it.

I'm not sure Joe agreed that this was the right next move for us, but he could see that it meant a lot to me, so it wasn't long after that conversation that he said, "Okay, Jill, if that's what you want. We'll try to have a baby." I went to see my doctor, who told me it might not happen right away. But to my surprise, just a month later, I started to feel the signs.

As secure as I felt the boys were in their relationship with me, I did worry that this new development might be a complication. If any part of me was questioning that I might not love them the same, I knew that would probably be true of the boys as well. New babies can be a tough adjustment for any kids, and I wanted to make sure Beau and Hunt continued to feel included on this journey. I wanted them to be excited about a new brother or sister, so rather than tell Joe, I went to Beau and Hunt first.

"I think I might be pregnant," I said. "But I don't want to tell Dad yet. Let's find out together." I drove them down to the Eckerd drugstore, and after we parked, I put on dark glasses and tied a scarf over my hair so that no one in the store would recognize me. The boys waited in the car, and I went in to buy an early pregnancy test. It was like a spy mission, and the boys were excited to have a secret just between us.

The test had to be taken in the morning, so first thing the next day, I took it—and yes, I was pregnant.

After Joe left to catch the train to D.C., I told the boys. "You should be the ones to tell your dad," I said.

That night, when Joe got home from work, Beau and Hunt could barely contain their excitement. "The boys have something to tell you," I said, and they exclaimed, "Dad! We're having a baby!" Joe's face lit up with pure joy. Standing there in the kitchen, he pulled all three of us into a hug, and as we embraced, I breathed a sigh of relief.

The next day, I called Val and asked her to meet me in the parking lot of the Food Fair grocery store, since it was between our two homes and the closest place we could meet and talk privately. She shrieked and hugged me when I gave her the news, and we popped open a bottle of champagne right there in the parking lot. Each of us only had a small taste, of course, but it was one of the most enjoyable sips of champagne I'd ever had.

At about 3:00 in the morning on June 8, 1981, I went into labor. I woke up Joe, but having been through three births already, he was unfazed. He knew better than I did how long these things took, especially first pregnancies. "Okay," he said when I woke him up. "Go back to sleep."

I couldn't go back to sleep. I figured I might as well be productive, so I got up, took a shower, and set my hair with hot rollers. What can I say? It was the '80s, and I didn't want to show up to one of the biggest moments of my life looking frazzled. As far as I could see, there was no reason not to look nice in the delivery room.

Soon after, I was doubled over in pain from the contractions while fixing my hair, thinking all the while, *What in God's name am I doing?* I put on my makeup and got dressed.

When we were ready to go, we woke up the boys and told them we'd find someone to stay over with them, but they refused, shouting, "No! We want to come, too!" The four of us piled into the car as my contractions began to pick up. I braced myself through the pain, squeezing my armrest for support. I felt like screaming and smashing my fist through the window, but I didn't want to scare the boys. I remembered how traumatic I found my mother's entire pregnancy, and how long those images had stuck with me. I held on to the dashboard while my knuckles turned white, breathing as deeply as I could to keep myself from moaning.

Despite my best efforts, I arrived at the emergency room a bit of a mess. My water broke in the car, so I was soaking wet—even my shoes squished as I walked—but my hair looked amazing! Joe and the boys helped me to the nurses' counter, where I told them between breaths that I was having a baby.

The nurse glanced up and blurted, "Wow, Joe Biden! Can I have your autograph?" I shot Joe a look that said, *You give that woman an autograph, and you are going to need your own hospital bed.* He flashed a Joe Biden smile but nervously mumbled back, "Well . . . maybe later."

The nurses started to prep me, and the moment they stuck a needle in my arm for an IV, Joe started to feel dizzy and sat down in a chair. Everyone immediately rushed from me to him, grabbing orange juice and smelling salts. *Don't worry about me,* I thought, *I'm just in labor!*

All throughout my pregnancy, I had said to Beau and Hunt, "This is your baby." We also told them they could choose the name. Out of the hundreds we discussed, the boys decided that for a girl, they liked the names Ashley and Colleen. Between the two choices, I preferred Ashley, so when the baby was born, we named her Ashley Blazer Biden—*Blazer* being the maiden name of my favorite grandmother, Grandmom Jacobs.

Ashley was a healthy weight—six pounds, eight ounces— but seemed impossibly small. She was somehow foreign and familiar, and all four of us were instantly in love. I could tell from day one that Joe was going to spoil her, and boy, did he ever. And Beau and Hunt adored her. They cradled her with so much tenderness, in a way that seemed unlikely from ten- and eleven-year-old boys. We brought her home together, and each of us knew our family was complete.

One of the hardest things about parenting an infant is that she is constantly changing. You struggle for weeks, or even months, to master how to feed this child, keep her from crying, or just get her to sleep. You find a trick—swaddle her just so, or sing her the right song, and you get a few blissful seconds of quiet. But then, as soon as you think you've got your footing, you wake up and she's a different baby. Now, she doesn't want the security of a wrapped blanket; she wants freedom to wiggle and thrash her arms about. Now, she hates her favorite food or toy, and giving it to her only makes her angry. It's jarring to have to adjust, but at the same time, you know the changes are coming. There are entire books dedicated to the ever-shifting nature of the skills, habits, and personality trends of little children. It's why parents of young kids will differentiate between a two-year-old and a two-and-a-half-year-old. A mere six months can be an enormous difference. We become flexible with babies and toddlers because we have to be.

As children grow older, however, we don't always expect to have to adapt so much—it catches us by surprise. We get used to the people we know, and it can be tempting to think they'll always be that way. When they grow into teenagers, or young adults, it's hard not to still see them as the little boy who caught snakes, or the little girl who loved ballet classes. You have to keep getting to know these new people—the same but different, with features that remind you of the children you used to know but with new ideas, new hopes, new problems, and new aspirations.

Joe never got to go on that journey with his baby daughter Naomi. He told stories about Neilia to the boys—there were years of stories to tell, after all—but he never mentioned their baby sister. Once, when someone asked him how many children he had, he answered, "Four." Simple questions like that occasionally have no right answer. It wasn't just that he'd lost a child he loved—he'd lost the chance to get to know her. All those memories of birthday cakes and late-night stories and learning to ride a bike and walking her down the aisle were stolen before they ever got to happen. She was a whole life that could have been. It was difficult for him to articulate that pain. In marriage, even a long one, there are some parts of yourself that you can only visit alone.

Shortly after Ashley's birth, we took her up to see the Hunters. I could tell they were genuinely grateful that we had visited, and they looked at her as if she were their own grandchild. But I know it must have been painful, too—another reminder of what they had lost.

One day, Joe said quietly, "Naomi would have been forty this year." Sometimes I marvel at Joe's strength. His life has been marked by cruel losses. Losing one child has been a nightmare for me. There are moments when I wonder if I will ever be the same. But to lose two children and his wife? And yet, Joe's faith in God, in life, and in hope remains. Despite it all, he finds joy. There is a Kahlil Gibran poem that reminds me of him:

> Then a woman said, Speak to us of Joy and
>   Sorrow.
> And he answered:
> Your joy is your sorrow unmasked.
> And the selfsame well from which your laughter
>   rises was oftentimes filled with your tears.
> And how else can it be?
> The deeper that sorrow carves into your being, the
>   more joy you can contain.

———

Ashley was just six years old when a first-grade classmate taunted her with the knowledge that Beau and Hunter weren't her "real brothers." I learned about it when I got a frantic call from one of Ashley's teachers, saying that Ashley was hysterical and they couldn't calm her down.

I was shocked—both that there were "mean girls" at age six and that they were talking about how the boys were not Ashley's "real" siblings. What did that even mean? What on earth could be more real than spending your life with two boys who looked out for you and fought with you over using the bathroom mirror? What was more real than sharing birthdays and Christmases and secrets that you hid from your parents? How could that bond be negated by a percentage of DNA?

We hadn't yet told Ashley about her dad's first marriage and the death of his wife and baby daughter. I thought it would be too scary, and I didn't want her dwelling on the thought of losing a parent or sibling. It didn't feel like the right time—she was too young—but now I had no choice but to tell her. I gently tried to explain, and Ashley burst into tears. It was horrible; as I'd expected, she didn't completely understand, but she was still upset by what she was learning.

This was a difficult moment for me as a mother. As we've seen over and over in our family, being in the public eye means people feel the need to weigh in on our personal relationships in a way they wouldn't for other families. But even those who don't deal with the spotlight must contend with unasked-for opinions on their family choices—what their relationships should be called, who counts as "real," and the implications of their parenting decisions. And this is on top of the self-questioning that we already do as parents.

I comforted Ashley that day and explained that this didn't change anything about our family, and I reassured her that she and her brothers were loved equally. At the same time, it made me think about the ways my relationships with each of my kids—though all built on unconditional love—were different.

I think most parents have moments of guilt over whether they've parented evenly; Joe and I certainly have. There were times when I've liked one of my children more—and less. Sometimes they had hobbies and talents we could connect over—and sometimes I just didn't get the stage they were in in their lives. There have been periods or moments when one of them needed me more—and I showered them with attention while the others got less. There were also times when *I* needed one of them more than I did the rest. So as parents, how do we live out that mantra every parent recites at some point or another: "I love you all the same"?

My relationship with Ashley did turn out to be different from the ones I had with the boys. Growing up with sisters, I was much more comfortable with the rituals of traditional girlhood—dolls and frilly dresses. Ashley and I could talk for hours—and still do. There is an honesty between us that I've come to depend on and could never replace. Where the boys were loud and dirty, I could sit with my little Ashley and play tea party all day. I once brought the boys to the symphony—an idea that seemed entirely sane to a new mom of preteen boys. I imagined them basking in the heartbreaking strings, whimsical woodwinds, and the boom of percussion. I had the romantic idea of sophisticated, cultured children who might rhapsodize on the nuances of Chopin and Tchaikovsky. The boys fell asleep almost as soon as the lights went down—and Joe couldn't even pretend to be sympathetic. "Who takes a ten-year-old to the symphony?" he teased. In Ashley, I finally had a child who would sit through art.

And with Ashley, I also saw the relationship I had with my father played back to me like a song stuck on repeat. There was no denying that she was my daughter: she tested me just like I tested my dad. And as a result, we fought all the time. I'd see her wearing a dress that was a little too sheer and say, "Go take that off! You're not wearing that to school." She'd change clothes, but then she'd bring the dress to school and change back into it there, just to defy me.

Joe also loves to tell the story about the battle of the head-bands. Back in the '80s, when everyone wore headbands, I had a whole rack of them in my bathroom. I had every color of the rainbow—plaid, gingham, with bows, without bows. It may sound strange now, but it was very fashionable at the time. Ashley would go in there and take them for herself, without asking. As Joe tells it, "I'd wake up in the morning, and there would be the two of them, going, 'It's *my* headband!' 'No, it's *my* headband!'" I can't say I agree completely with this retelling, but I admit I was frustrated by my constantly disappearing hair accessories.

During Ashley's teenage years, I kept a pair of running shoes by the door. Whenever she and I would get into an argument, I'd put on those shoes and go running to calm myself down. We argued so much, I became a marathon runner. It wasn't the same with Joe; he doted on her, and their personalities never clashed the way ours did. Perhaps it was a mother-daughter thing, but not one I recognized at all. My relationship with my mom was so different.

"Believe me," I'd tell her, "when you have a child, I hope she's a girl, so she can put you through what you've put me through."

All of this meant I suddenly had a new appreciation for my father. This child was, obviously, his perfect revenge. Obstinate and strong-willed, she'd come in after her curfew or sometimes cut school. She was stubborn and rebellious, like I was, though she never got into any serious trouble. I tried to channel my mother's parenting—calm, coolheaded, always nurturing—but it was my father's style I reverted to most often, one of tough love.

While my relationship with Ashley was different from the ones I had with the boys, it was just that—different, not more or less. I saw myself in Beau and Hunter, too, and my relationship with each of them was unique.

Beau had my sense of humor completely. Whenever he started in his chopped way, "Mom, Mom, Mom," I knew something funny was about to come out of his mouth. The two of us were the only ones who would pick on Joe, and he loved that I would say things to his dad that no one else dared. But it wasn't just our personality traits that overlapped—with his blond hair and blue eyes, people always remarked on how we looked alike. "You take after your mom," strangers would tell us when we were together—and we would smile and share a secret look, never correcting them.

In Hunt, I had a fellow scholar and writer. He loves books and poetry—just like his English-professor mother. He's the one I want to call when I finish a heartbreaking novel or need a recommendation of a good book to read. He has insight and wisdom and makes me see things through a different prism. And though he's my most courageous child, I also feel the most protective of him, because I know he shares my guarded emotional side. We're not the politicians of the family, but we know how to put our strengths to work for what we believe. He came with me to New Orleans, L.A., to provide aid after Hurricane Katrina, and we visited the Kibera slum in Kenya together. Like me, he can't see others suffering without wanting to step in. When he sees someone hurting, he finds a way to help.

Biology or not, I'm a part of all of my kids—and they are a part of me. I've loved them each in different ways, and I've often loved them unevenly. My love is constantly undulating, moving and changing and growing, flowing to where it's needed and back again. And in the end, though it is uneven, it equals out.

At least that's my hope. And I have reason to believe it has worked. Hunter once alleviated some of my fears. "You know, Mom," he told me, "I never doubted that you loved us the same as you did Ashley." When I asked him why, he said, "Because you yelled at her just like you yelled at us."

9

DISCOVERING MY VOICE

I was never a natural as a "political spouse." As an introvert, I preferred to stay in the background. Events that Joe and I attended together usually unfolded much like my first political picnic. He was completely in his element—talking to everyone he could, earnestly listening to stories, and connecting with total strangers. He was witty and gregarious, and I loved watching him glow when he got the chance to discuss an issue he cared about or hear an opposing perspective. Meanwhile, I was much quieter and more reticent to engage, so when strangers approached me at events, I had a hard time leaving my reserved self behind. This is a dilemma faced by any introvert married to an extrovert, but here it was magnified because of Joe's position.

People often misinterpreted my shyness, assuming it was something more intentional, a haughty snobbery. Some seemed nervous and intimidated to meet me, apparently unable to imagine that I was nervous and intimidated myself. Perhaps they saw me as a polished senator's wife with her life in pristine order: I was young, with gorgeous children, and on the arm of a man who was quite a catch. There was no denying we made a picture-perfect Christmas card, but in truth, I rarely felt as confident as I tried to look. I, too, scoured the magazines looking for dieting and makeup tips. I, too, wondered if I was pretty enough, successful enough, a good enough mother. I felt inadequate at times, in the way that women are often conditioned to do.

After a few months of attending events as Senator Biden's wife, it became obvious that my social limitations were getting in my way. I was going to have to figure out how to warm up in crowds. I started slowly, making myself initiate conversations. This proved easier to do in rural areas, with the older, grandmotherly women who often came to Joe's events, and more difficult among the crowds of professionals and politicos in Wilmington. But little by little, I forced myself through my discomfort. I tried to be curious rather than anxious. And I found that, after playing the part for a little while, I became more comfortable with it.

Just as I was starting to feel like I was getting the hang of this political wife thing, Joe upped the ante. He'd been invited to give a speech at the Belle-Everett Dinner, a big annual fundraising event in Kent County, and when it turned out he had a scheduling conflict, he asked if I'd be willing to step in.

I didn't want to give any speeches, anytime, anywhere— just the thought of doing so made me so nervous I felt sick. Even though this was a political dinner where the crowd was sure to be friendly and welcoming, I couldn't bear the thought of standing up at a podium and talking in front of hundreds of people. Sure, I spoke in front of my students every day—I had returned to work by then—but in the classroom, I was in control. My kids looked up to me, and I was confident I knew what I was talking about. A political dinner was a totally different kind of environment.

Worse, these people didn't want me—they were hoping for Joe, someone all of Delaware knew as an excellent orator. On the drive to Kent County, I kept reading and rereading the speech that one of Joe's staff members had written for me. I don't know whether it was pure nerves or all that reading in the car, but by the time Val and I arrived at the dinner, I felt nauseated.

Val, always my political mentor, gave me a pep talk in the parking lot—and I would have given anything to just absorb her positivity and confidence. *Jill, you got this!* she assured me. After it was finally over, all I remembered was staring down at the sheaf of papers in my shaking hands and reading the words in a whispery voice. I got through that speech by sheer will—because I had to—but at home, I told Joe that was the last speech for me. I would stick to high school lectures.

In fact, that was the last big speech I gave for a while. It wasn't until 1987, when Joe launched his first presidential campaign, that I agreed to get behind a podium again. Joe was in the middle of one of the most high-profile events of his political career—the Senate confirmation hearings for Supreme Court nominee Robert Bork—and he wasn't able to travel as much as a presidential campaign would usually require. So instead of skipping around the country to Iowa and New Hampshire, he sent me.

I believe that in good relationships, there has to be a balance between knowing who you are—not compromising on the essential things that make you *you*—and being willing to grow as a person. On the one hand, you marry someone (hopefully) knowing their weaknesses and limitations, and loving them for the complete person they are—blemishes and all. But on the other hand, that isn't an excuse to be static. We have to keep evolving. There's a difference between expecting your partner to understand that you are not, by nature, a fastidious cleaner and using that as an excuse to never once do the dishes. We do change for our spouses. We try to be worthy of their love, just as they try to be worthy of ours. Good marriages push us—not to become someone else but to become the best version of ourselves.

Joe has always seen strength in me that I haven't always seen in myself. He knew that a lot of my hang-ups with public speaking came from insecurity. But he also knew that I had the fortitude to face the challenge, and he wanted to give me a chance to use my voice, so that year, he asked me to hit the campaign trail. "Jilly," he said, "I need you . . . and I know you can do it."

It was nerve-racking every time I took the podium, but I discovered something on the campaign trail: Speaking wasn't as horrible when I actually wanted to be there. I believed Joe was the best candidate. I was passionate about telling his story and convincing people that he was up for the job. It wasn't just an obligation to be out there—to stand in his place and share my vision—it was a privilege.

Years later, I would hold him accountable to his best self as well. In 2008, there were a lot of reasons not to run for president, and Joe had been going back and forth with his decision. When the question of another run had come up in years past, we weren't ready. But after almost eight years of George W. Bush, with two wars hanging over Americans' heads, there was one thing that was clear to me: Joe needed to run. So we called a family meeting, and I basically told him it was decided—he was ready, we were ready, and we weren't taking "maybe next time" for an answer.

When Joe declared as a candidate that year, our whole family went into action. It was, after all, the Biden way, ever since Val ran his impossible Senate bid. From the time the boys and Ashley were little, they campaigned along with their father. They went everywhere with us—to the state fair, the picnics, the pancake breakfasts, the parades. Beau loved it, eagerly sticking out his skinny arm to shake hands with voters left and right—that was how I knew he would follow in Joe's footsteps as a politician. But Hunter and Ashley were happy to be out there, too—beaming with pride for their father, ready to step up to whatever was needed from them.

In Joe's previous Senate campaigns, I'd shake hands at coffee gatherings and senior centers and answer people's questions one-on-one, but I didn't do much in the way of "stumping." That changed in the 2008 campaign—particularly after Barack Obama selected Joe as his running mate.

Suddenly, Beau, Hunter, Ashley, and I all started traveling separately around the country, making appearances and giving speeches. The crowds were much bigger than any I'd spoken to before—thousands of people, sometimes in vast arenas—and I had to get used to that very quickly. It still wasn't coming naturally to me, and I still struggled to channel the easygoing demeanor that people can connect with. One reporter noted in a story that I was "not the most polished political performer, reading carefully from her speeches." But I didn't give up. I practiced hard and spent time getting tips from a professional speaking coach. I never got completely used to these appearances, but I came to appreciate them for what they were—an opportunity to use my voice for good.

After Barack and Joe won the election, I knew that the four years—and hopefully eight—in the White House would go quickly. And I knew that I had a chance to be a voice for some of the people in my life who often went unheard, such as military families and community college students. This was one of the biggest platforms in the world, and I told myself on day one, *I will never waste this opportunity.* I had come a long way from my whispery, fearful speech at the Belle-Everett Dinner.

Marriages, like most important things in life, have seasons—"a time for every purpose under heaven," as Ecclesiastes tells us. And in those early days of our marriage, I found purpose in my role as a mom. This purpose was renewed again after Ashley was born, but eventually, I would feel the winds shift. As a mother, I often found myself living for everyone else, putting their needs first, and fostering their success. My own mother did this all of her life. Many women—and many men, for that matter—find great fulfillment in that role. Being a stay-at-home parent, working full-time to raise children and build a home with all of the mundane and miraculous moments in between, can be one of the most rewarding pursuits of one's life. But it is also a job, a very difficult one at times, and like all jobs, it may not be a good fit for everyone or for the long term. As the days passed doing laundry or planning dinners, I found myself longing to be back in a classroom.

As a mother of three and the wife of a senator, working full-time wasn't exactly the simplest path. Add night school and a master's program to that equation, and some would find it downright ill-advised. We had help, of course, especially from a wonderful woman by the name of Helen, who babysat Ashley. Were Joe a different man, he might have encouraged me to put my career aside. But I couldn't just be his wife. I had always wanted to pursue a career, and though I was happy to have taken time off to be with the kids, that desire still burned within me. I had my own dreams and ambitions, and Joe didn't love me in spite of that—he loved me because of it.

Ruth Bader Ginsburg once commented in an interview, "You can't have it all, all at once. Who—man or woman—has it all, all at once? Over my lifespan I think I have had it all. But in different periods of time things were rough. And if you have a caring life partner, you help the other person when that person needs it." I knew—and Joe knew—that I couldn't be the wife or mother I wanted to be if I didn't follow my own path. So, following two years at home after Ashley's birth, I went back to teaching.

Over the years, I've heard so many people talk about teachers in a way that doesn't reflect the reality of teaching that I know at all. They think it's a job for people without ambitions, that teaching doesn't take a lot of skill, and that teachers have short hours and summers off. I've taught in a lot of different environments, but one thing is always the same: teaching is rewarding, but it's a tremendous challenge, too.

I began my career teaching ninth- and tenth-grade English but left after Joe and I got married to spend a couple of years at home with the boys. When I returned to teaching, my next job was working as a reading specialist. After a brief stint at Concord High School, the state moved me to Claymont High.

Decades after *Brown v. Board of Education,* Delaware was still struggling to desegregate its schools, and Wilmington students had sued for integration and won. The result was an influx of new black students at Claymont from schools that were underfunded and stretched thin.

Many of these new students were behind on basic skills, and my job was to help them catch up with their peers in reading. The experience taught me just how difficult it is to make up for lost learning time. As research has shown, those first few years in school lay a foundation for the rest of our education—indeed, for the rest of our lives—and without a strong start, my students had significant obstacles to overcome.

I worked at Claymont until Ashley was born in 1981. Then, after taking my second two-year break from teaching to care for her, I took a job at a psychiatric hospital—one of the most intensely difficult jobs I've ever had.

When I started, I had fifteen or twenty kids as students—many of whom were adolescents who'd tried to commit suicide. I saw kids who were anorexic, and others who were dealing with serious drug addictions. Some were cutting themselves, which was something I'd never heard of before. Most were suffering from depression and anxiety, and some were emotionally flat from prescription drugs. Whenever students got out of control, we had to send them to padded rooms for time-outs. There were so many kids dealing with so much pain.

I taught history and English, while another teacher taught math and science. We worked to make these kids' education as seamless as possible; I'd contact the students' teachers to get their curricula and then work individually with each one to keep up with his or her regular schoolwork. We taught in groups, but

I tried to give them as much one-on-one time as I could. My students had been through so much, and I felt frustrated that I couldn't help them more. Still, when I trudged home at the end of the day, I knew I'd made a difference in their lives—at least some of them. I'll never forget seeing one girl outside the hospital a few months after I left. She was with a group of friends, and I didn't say hello because I didn't want her to have to explain how she knew me. But seeing her laugh with her friends put a smile on my face. After such a difficult road to recovery, I was grateful to see her enjoying a simple teenage moment.

There's something profoundly optimistic about teaching. We are taking the best of what humans have to give—lifetimes of knowledge, wisdom, craft, and art—and handing it over to the next generation, with the hope that they will continue to build, continue to make our world better. It's a conversation with our past and future selves at once, a way of saying, *Look what we've done! Now what will you do with it?*

And it can be all-consuming. We spend our free time planning lessons and researching materials. We have to keep on top of the latest research on brain development and education styles. Teaching at the psychiatric hospital was my first job in which all of my students were dealing with mental illness—but it certainly wasn't the first time I'd had to figure out how to help students with eating disorders, anxiety, depression, or destructive behavior. Teachers often have to be counselors, social workers, mediators, and family. I know so many who spend their own money to make sure their kids have all the tools they need for the year. The truth is, the time we spend actually teaching sentence structure or equations or chemical compounds is only a fraction of the job.

In fact, for a lot of us, we never really leave the classroom behind. Whether it's cooking dinner, buying groceries, or watching the latest TV show—there's always a part of you that's thinking about your students. Everywhere you go, and in everything you do, you carry them with you.

So why do we do it? We do it for that spark in a student's eye when an idea falls into place. We do it for the moment when a student realizes she's capable of more than she'd thought. For the chance to hold a student's hand as she begins to explore this wild, incredible world through books and equations and historical accounts. We do it because we love it.

I loved it. And I still do.

Classrooms are like little communities: after so much time together, there are inside jokes, rivalries, obligations to each other, and, hopefully, trust. At the beginning of a semester, my students are often shy, closed up. But as time passes, they begin to share their stories. They talk about their fears and let the rest of us know what they're struggling with or rejoicing over. They begin to be vulnerable with one another and offer to lend a hand when someone needs study help or a ride to work. It's especially true in community colleges, where students are older and used to dealing with hardships. Watching them grow and change reminds me to keep pushing myself as well. They remind me that no one is so strong that they don't need help.

One afternoon at NOVA, I was telling my class that I'd have to miss our next session for personal reasons. By that point in the term, we had all become close, and no one seemed to have any real filters anymore. They all began shouting, "Where are you going, Dr. B.?"

So I told them. "My sister Jan is having a stem cell transplant,"

I said. "Today is her first treatment, and she'll have to stay in the same hospital room for six weeks." My other sisters and I had come up with a schedule to stay with her so she wouldn't have to be alone through the treatment. Ever the big sister, I was doing my best to wear a brave face. Everything was going to be fine, I kept telling Bonny, Kelly, and Kim. I brought out my reassuring smile for my family as much as I could, but standing in front of my class, I suddenly lost my composure. I had to pause, as the next words caught in my throat. "I just . . . need to be with her."

I quickly faced the whiteboard so the students wouldn't see the tears filling my eyes.

When I turned back around, every single student was standing. They made a line and came up to hug me, one by one. At that moment, I knew just how much I needed them. Hugging each student, I realized this, too, was my family.

There have been a few times in my life where I have felt fate revealing something crucial to me—where there's been an instant of clarity, and I've known exactly what to do next. Some of these moments have been dramatic, like deciding to accept Joe's fifth proposal. But the time in 1993 when a friend of mine called to tell me about Delaware Tech was not one of those moments.

She called just a few weeks after she had left Brandywine High, where we had been working together. I had taken a job there a few years before, after my time teaching at the psychiatric hospital. "Jill," she said, "you've got to come by. I promise you, you would love it." I wasn't sure. I liked my classes at

Brandywine High School, and the notion of making the leap to teaching adults in college was intimidating. Still, the idea of no longer having to serve on cafeteria duty *was* enticing, so I visited the Del Tech campus, met with the dean, and eventually accepted a job there.

My friend was right. I liked teaching high school, but something clicked for me at Del Tech. I saw so much courage and determination in my students. Some of them were coming from families who had never dreamed they would have a child go to college. Some of them were looking for a second chance after making mistakes or dropping out of a four-year school. Some of them were older, having not been able to take that traditional path, having spent years working and saving and dreaming of the day they could get their degrees and make a better life for themselves.

Working with community college students was unlike anything I'd done up to that point. I got to know my students in a way I hadn't in past settings. When we talked about literature, they had life experience to share. They brought diverse perspectives to our studies—of travels and jobs and families and challenges they had overcome. And they wanted to be there— *really* wanted to be there. They cared about education in a way that people who have never had to fight just to be in class, who have never skipped dinner so they could save up for tuition, just couldn't understand. It was such an honor to be the person to walk them through their studies, to give them the key that would unlock something life-changing.

They often needed extra help and attention, but I also found myself giving life advice, or just being a pair of ears to listen. I knew that some of them would come to class hungry—some were working two and three jobs in addition to school, just to stay afloat. So I started bringing breakfast bars to class, offering them to whoever needed one. I put a container in front of the classroom so students could bring bottles of water, or a pack of Ramen noodles, or a sports drink to share with their classmates. They helped each other, because so many of them knew what it was like to be barely getting by.

The challenges my students faced were different from mine in many ways—having to get across town without a car, having to choose between paying the utility bill and buying a textbook. But in a lot of ways, our challenges were similar—I knew what it was like to juggle childcare, a job, and night classes. I knew what it was like to be the oldest person in a class, feeling like you're always behind. I knew how frustrating it could be to look ahead and see a degree that is still so far away. It took me fifteen years to get my graduate degrees, so I saw myself in those students. And I knew at that point that I would be a community college professor for the rest of my career.

I've had that job for a quarter century now—first for fifteen years at Del Tech, then for the past decade at Northern Virginia Community College. When Barack and Joe won the election in 2008, I was still at Del Tech, and everyone assumed I'd stop teaching and become a full-time Second Lady. But not only did I want to keep teaching, I was being recruited by the dean at NOVA, Jimmie McClellan. Every few weeks, he'd send me funny emails essentially saying, "Hi! You don't know me, but I think you'd really love our school. We'd love to have you teach here."

I knew that as Second Lady, I'd be swept up into the political world—which was fine. I also knew that, just like before, when I took those years off to look after the kids, I would be unhappy if that were my whole life. Teaching is my internal compass; I can always count on it to steer me in the right direction. But could I really continue to do it as Joe assumed the role of vice president?

Cathy Russell, a trusted friend and my new chief of staff, didn't think so. "Jill, are you crazy?" she said after the election. "You can't do this—it's too much."

"If I don't teach, I'm not going to be happy," I replied. She tried to talk me out of my decision, but in the end, it really was that simple. So we set up a meeting with Dean McClellan, and as soon as I walked onto the campus at NOVA, I knew it was right. "Cathy," I said, "I'm going to do this." I accepted a job for that semester and began teaching after the inauguration in late January.

For the Secret Service, this was a whole new territory. At first, they wanted to be in the classroom with me, but I couldn't have them sitting right there in the front row—the students would be too intimidated. I hoped not only that my students would not notice there were Secret Service agents nearby, but also that they wouldn't even realize I was the Second Lady. And as unlikely as it seems, many of them didn't.

So the agents dressed like college students, and even carried backpacks—of course, the backpacks had their "equipment" in them rather than books. The average age of students at NOVA is twenty-eight, so the agents didn't look out of place. There was a seating area just down the hall from my classroom, and they'd sit there while I taught, alongside students who were studying and reading—and no one was any the wiser. Their ability and willingness to do their jobs while seamlessly blending in was remarkable.

We had decided in advance that when students signed up for classes, mine would be listed as being taught by *staff*, rather than *Dr. Biden*. On the first day of class, I'd write my name on the board and say, "Hi, I'm Jill Biden—but just call me Dr. B." The vast majority of my students are first-generation arrivals from other countries, and for many of them, English is their second language. Most didn't notice the *Biden* name, and if they did, they didn't put together that I was married to the vice president.

Every so often, a student would figure it out. She'd raise her hand and say, "Excuse me, may I ask you a personal question?"

"Nope!" I'd say, and change the subject.

Once, a student came blowing into my office, exclaiming, "Dr. B.! I saw you last night on the television! I said to my mother, 'Mom! Mom! Look! That's my English teacher with *Michelle Obama!*'"

I just looked at her, smiling. She went on, "Then my mom rolled her eyes at me and said, 'That's not your English teacher. That's the Second Lady!'" This student had gone the whole semester not having a clue who I was, but I laughed and admitted it. She clapped a hand over her mouth, her eyes wide, and laughed, too.

Once, a student in her midsixties—a woman who was studying to become a drug counselor—came up and whispered in my ear, "I know who you are. And no one else here does."

I looked at her out of the corner of my eye and whispered back, "That's right. And we're gonna keep it that way."

Our jobs can be powerful avenues to channel our passions, but they don't have to be the only way we make a difference. It's not always about our title; sometimes it's about following our strengths, no matter where they lead us.

Joe's passion is being a voice for people who are marginalized and disenfranchised. He has spent most of his career accomplishing this as a politician, but even now as a civilian, he hasn't slowed down. Beau had that same spark that pushed him into the spotlight, and he used it to shine a light on child mistreatment and other abuses of power.

Ashley's strength has always been organizing around philanthropy and social justice. When she was just six or seven years old, she became very passionate about dolphins getting caught in tuna fishing nets, so she went to Joe and asked how she could help. And soon, she was making her way around the halls of the Senate, telling Joe's colleagues about how we needed to do a better job keeping the dolphins safe. Later, she took up the cause of kids who had been treated unfairly in our justice system. I'm so proud of the work she's been doing with the Delaware Center for Justice, which fights for fairness in our court and prison systems.

Hunter's gift is his limitless empathy and drive. After he graduated high school, he went to Belize and taught at-risk kids with the Jesuit Volunteer Corps (JVC), learning about education inequities and poverty. In college and after, he continued to work with the JVC, this time in Portland, Oregon, helping at a shelter for homeless men.

For a long time, I thought my strengths were limited to what I could do in the classroom. But, once again, Joe knew better.

A few years after the '88 campaign, a close friend of mine was diagnosed with breast cancer. She and I were both in our early forties, and it was a shock to my system that someone so close to me—someone so young—was that ill. Then, another friend confided that she, too, had been diagnosed with breast cancer. Then another. Then another. In 1993, no fewer than four of my friends were in various stages of the disease.

I couldn't get over how rampant breast cancer was among young, otherwise healthy women. I'd visit my friends and drive them to appointments, but I became desperate to do more. One afternoon, I stopped by to see my friend Winnie at her home. She was pale and painfully thin, with a scarf wrapped around her bare head. We sat talking on her couch as her hospice nurse stood by, and I struggled not to cry in front of her. I just couldn't believe that this wonderful person—a mother of three children who adored and needed her—was about to die.

When I got home that afternoon, I said, "Joe, I have to do something. This is happening to too many people." I was no activist and never had been, but the weight of this situation was pushing me to become one. How could I, someone so connected to the powerful world of D.C., with a husband who refused to stand by and allow injustice to spread, do nothing? As I was taught growing up, "To whom much is given, much will be required." Joe agreed. "You're right," he told me. "Get to work." That was the beginning of the Biden Breast Health Initiative.

I didn't quite know where to begin or what to do. But given my background, Joe encouraged me to focus on education. He helped me invite a group of doctors, nurses, health advocates, and breast cancer survivors to our house to talk about what we could do. We decided to focus on Delaware high schoolers, to teach them about breast health, self-exams, and healthy habits, and soon a small group of us began visiting high schools around the state. And while I leaned on Joe in the beginning, I was eventually able to step up and lead. It was teaching, after all, and that was where I knew I could shine. We educated young women about early detection and showed them how to perform self-examinations. We made sure medical professionals were there to answer questions. And we sent students home to spread the message to their families and friends about healthy habits—getting screenings, eating nutritiously, and never smoking.

We went into nearly every high school in Delaware, and in some places, our program was seen as radical. It was the early '90s, and some parents felt that talking about breasts at school, even in the context of health, was too much. At one high school in Dover, girls had to take permission slips home for a parent's signature just to attend the class. That alone was evidence that our work was needed, if only to demystify the topic of breast health.

In addition to the education program, we offered three $5,000 scholarships—one in each of Delaware's three counties—to students who were going into health-related careers. And all the funding for these initiatives came from one fantastic event held every year at Chez Nicole Hair and Nail Salon, in Wilmington. All the nail techs would donate their time, and people would come and pay fifty dollars for a manicure or pedicure, with all the proceeds going to the Biden Breast Health Initiative. There was always a large number of breast cancer survivors there, enjoying the music, the food, and the feeling of community. So many women wanted to come that we had to start a waiting list.

In her book *The Cancer Journals*, Audre Lorde talked about her struggle with breast cancer and her mastectomy. She eventually lost her battle to the disease, though it was liver cancer that took her life. But the book is about much more than a diagnosis; it's a beautiful reflection on life, fear, and survival. In it, she wrote, "I realize that if I wait until I am no longer afraid to act, write, speak, be, I'll be sending messages on a Ouija board, cryptic complaints from the other side. When I dare to be powerful, to use my strength in the service of my vision, then it becomes less important whether or not I am unafraid."

We like to think that our personalities are immutable, a constant throughout our lives. But we evolve with each victory, each defeat, each step forward, each scar. The truth is that we can't know who we will become. Sometimes I look at pictures of young Jill Jacobs and wonder: *Who was that girl?*

Life changes all of us. And the only way I know to keep what we have, even as we evolve, is to find opportunities to grow together. Because in the midst of our transformations, we can hold on to one important thing: the trust we have in each other.

I've had a mixed relationship with the public eye over the years. But between campaigning and the Biden Breast Health Initiative, between my years as a teacher and my public work as Second Lady, I've seen beyond my introverted nature and discovered how important it is to use my voice. With the trust of Joe and my family, I've learned to set aside my fears, and I've dared to be powerful.

10

BECOMING A DAUGHTER

Get out of this room! Get *out!*" I shouted, rushing between the priest administering last rites and my husband's hospital bed. I yell so rarely that the sound of my voice surprised me almost as much as it did the priest. I'd left for one hour—just trying to make sure the rest of the family was taken care of while we waited for Joe's test results—and what do I come back to, but the hospital making preparations for his death? This was impossible. Joe was needed too much by our boys, who couldn't lose another parent; by our little girl, who thought he hung the moon; by *me*.

It was February of 1988, and I'd been teaching one of my English classes at Claymont High when I learned Joe was ill. Through the glass pane of the classroom door, I could see the principal standing just outside with a fellow teacher and friend, Betty Jo. They opened the door, and Betty Jo said, "We got a call, Jill. You need to go home." I looked at them, confused. "It's your husband. Something has happened."

I had a sinking feeling as I drove through the cold streets of our Montchan neighborhood, but at the same time, I couldn't imagine what would be so urgent. Joe was young and healthy. He had been in Rochester, New York, the night before to give a speech and seemed fine when I'd last spoken to him. What could have happened so quickly?

I walked into our bedroom with fear aching in the back of my throat and found Joe lying on the bed. He was awake but not quite there; his skin was literally gray, as if he were slowly becoming an old family portrait. I'd never seen him—or anyone—look like that, and knew instantly that something was seriously wrong. "We have to get him to the hospital now," I told his brother Frankie and his assistant, Tom Lewis. We helped Joe down to the car, and he kept saying he was okay; but, barely able to walk on his own, he clearly wasn't.

Saint Francis Healthcare was the closest hospital, right in the center of Wilmington, and as soon as we pulled up at the emergency room entrance, a phalanx of doctors came flying over, white coats fluttering. They brought Joe inside, and I stayed with him until the doctors decided to do a CT scan to try to find out why his head hurt so badly. While Joe was having tests done, I raced home to check on the kids. Ashley was only six, and I didn't want her to come home from kindergarten to an empty house. Beau was away at college, but Hunt was a high school senior, still living at home, and I wanted to let him know right away what was going on.

I hurried back to the hospital and found a nurse waiting at a desk outside the door of Joe's room. She was reading charts, but as I approached, she paused to look up casually and say, "Oh, don't go in right now, Mrs. Biden. They're giving him the last rites."

Everything was spinning out of control. Dizzy from a cocktail of adrenaline and fear, that's when I rushed into the room, screaming at the priest.

As it turned out, Joe had undergone a spinal tap following his CT scan. And that spinal tap confirmed how serious the problem was: there was blood in Joe's spinal column.

He had suffered an aneurysm.

Now that we had a diagnosis, Joe's brother Jimmy went into action, trying to find the best surgeon possible. There was a highly recommended doctor in Canada, one in Virginia, and one at Walter Reed hospital in Washington, D.C. The doctors were firm that Joe couldn't fly, as the change in air pressure could kill him, so we decided to transport him by ambulance down to Dr. Gene George at Walter Reed.

As I watched the EMTs lift Joe into the ambulance, the silence felt heavy. Sometimes, the only way I know how to deal with the unthinkable—and losing Joe was unthinkable—is to joke. "Well, you've really ruined Valentine's Day," I chided as I climbed in next to him. It was Friday, February 12, and we had planned to go away for a romantic weekend. Instead, we were now part of a caravan racing down I-95, with state police, a medical team, and our entire family, including Val, Jimmy, Mom Mom, and Dada. As we sped down the quiet highway, it started to snow. "If you die, I'm moving to North Carolina," I added. "I'm done with this winter business." Joe laughed faintly.

When we arrived at the hospital around 11:00 p.m., Dr. George was waiting with bad news: he'd have to operate as soon as they could pull together a surgery team. Joe had a bleeding aneurysm, and it could kill him if not treated immediately.

The Walter Reed staff took us into a conference room, and

we all began frantically discussing the surgery, next steps, and everything we would have to do. The Bidens would come together to solve this problem, but I found myself shrinking away. The room felt like it was closing in on me, and I made an excuse to leave. I found an empty room down the hall and sank to the floor. I felt like I'd been in the center of a thunderstorm, and the sudden quiet made me feel both grateful and empty. "Please, God," I prayed aloud. "Let him live."

Joe's aneurysm came on the heels of a very difficult year. When we entered the presidential race in 1987, I wasn't sure what to think. At first, it wasn't even clear if it *was* a presidential run; Joe initially intended to test the waters for the following cycle. But he'd had such a positive initial reaction from people all over the country that it seemed like the right time. As enthusiasm grew, as more and more talented, smart people joined our team, it felt like we were on an unstoppable train. Even though I had reservations about the timing—were the kids ready? Was I ready?—I believed deeply in Joe as a candidate.

At the time, Joe was balancing two incredibly difficult jobs: running for president and heading up the Robert Bork nomination hearings as chair of the Senate Judiciary Committee. On the political side, he was trying to share a vision of a better America in small towns across the country. On the Senate side, he was making a delicate legal case to protect the Supreme Court—a case he would go on to win.

While he was torn between these two worlds, I spent months traveling and speaking on his behalf, opening up our house to campaign workers, and doing everything I could to support the effort. Still, our lives had to continue. I was teaching, Hunt was finishing up his senior year and preparing for college, Beau was adjusting to his freshman year at the University of Pennsylvania, and our little Ashley was just getting started. It was an exhausting time, but I knew Joe had the ability, intelligence, and integrity to be a transformational president.

For his entire political life, Joe had been known for his integrity. Time and time again, he'd stood up to moneyed interests or gone against those in his own party when he thought it was the right thing to do. He was so honest, he occasionally got himself in trouble for speaking the truth rather than giving politic sound bites. So when he was accused of plagiarism during his presidential bid, it was not only politically damaging, it was *personally* devastating. Joe had a choice: He could fight these charges in the public arena every day, battling a media frenzy, distracting and perhaps even compromising his work on the Judiciary Committee; or he could leave the race and focus on keeping Judge Bork from being elevated to the highest court, with consequences that would last for generations. He made the choice to put his presidential bid aside.

When Joe left the race in September of 1987, it was one of the few times I cried unabashedly, alone in my bedroom, with the door shut tight. At that moment, I got a call from Mom Mom. When she heard how upset I was, she said, "I'll come right over."

Since our family was often scrutinized, we were extremely protective of each other. Val in particular had become one of my best friends, and because she knew how much I loved Joe, she was one of the only people I could be honest with about my everyday frustrations.

But as is true with most families, the dynamics were complicated at times. Mom Mom and I were both strong-willed and opinionated—we both wanted what was best for Joe and the kids, but we didn't always agree on what that was. And though all of the Bidens treated me with love and respect, there were times when I still felt like I was just the woman Joe married. It was my own insecurity. I was always trying to be self-sufficient in a group of people who believed "if you have to ask, it's too late." I was still a bit reserved, a trait that was difficult to shoehorn into this boisterous, affectionate family.

But when Mom Mom came over that day, all I could think was, *I can't do this alone.* In that moment, I was so grateful for her, so grateful that she hadn't let me be strong or independent. I didn't know how much I needed her until I was falling apart in her arms. And there, in my bedroom, she held me as I wept.

Our doctor told us there was a fifty-fifty chance Joe wouldn't survive surgery. He also said that it was even more likely that Joe would have permanent brain damage if he survived. And if any part of his brain would be adversely affected, it would be the area that governed speech.

Even after Joe survived the surgery, brain function intact, we still weren't in the clear. It would be a messy recovery, and he would end up needing more surgeries after he suffered a second aneurysm while recovering at home.

In those first few days at Walter Reed, the entire family huddled again, terrified, in a conference room to discuss Joe's care. Val and Jimmy were debating what was next—who needed to be called, how we would handle his staff, which course of treatment was best. Both had strong opinions about what was best for their brother and were completely intent on directing the next move. I sat there silently, listening to them go back and forth like I was stuck behind one-way glass. When they started calling in doctors to issue their orders, I'd finally had enough. "Wait a minute!" I shouted. "He's *my* husband. I should be making the decision here."

Everyone froze, shocked by my outburst.

"She's right," Mom Mom said. "This is Jill's decision."

Looking back, I shouldn't have been surprised that she stood up for me. Mom Mom had always said husbands and wives had a special obligation beyond the rest of the family. But still, I didn't expect her to side with me over her kids, and it was probably even more difficult to take a back seat herself.

In that moment, I truly felt I was a Biden. And I belonged at that table, making decisions that would affect us all.

Years later, at Beau's bedside as he valiantly fought the cancer that would take his life, I thought of Mom Mom and that moment at Walter Reed. Beau's illness was excruciating, and it was agonizing to watch him struggle through chemotherapy and operation after operation. For so many years throughout my son's childhood, I had taken his temperature, I had given him his medicine, I had nursed him back to health. It was me he came to when he broke his arm or cut his leg. The doctors turned to me to ask if I wanted him to have stitches, a splint, an antibiotic. And now, in the greatest struggle of his life, I wanted to sit the doctors down and demand to know our options. Who else could know better what he needed? Who else could make those decisions other than someone who had watched him grow up?

But there was only one answer: Hallie. She was his wife.

It wasn't my job anymore—it wasn't my place. It hurt like hell, but that's the way of it. Our roles within our families change and shift and evolve, and we have to learn to let go.

I've often thought of how difficult it must have been for Joe to be a father when he was coping with the loss of Neilia and Naomi. Parents are supposed to be the ones with the answers, the ones who can tell you that everything is going to be okay. But how do you make your children believe that things will work out when you aren't so sure that they will—when you have no answers, only sadness and confusion? Sometimes I feel like I've forgotten how to be the mom after the death of my son. I worry about my children worrying about me, feeling like they need to be the strong ones. It's not the right order of things. How can I be there for my children when I feel so lost?

There's a Hemingway quote that has stayed with me since I first read it: "The world breaks every one and afterward many are strong at the broken places." It always makes me think of Joe.

There have been many times when he was broken by life— too many. But he's always found a way to put himself back together. It's not that he doesn't have vulnerabilities; everyone does. He does, however, possess a strength that can seem surreal. It's one of the main reasons I married him. I wanted a partner who could shoulder all of life's disappointments, tragedies, and sorrows with me. But, my God, I never imagined what that would actually mean. I never thought that my life would plunge to such dark depths or reach such glorious heights.

I recently read that the common wisdom that broken bones

heal to be stronger than before is a myth. Calcium deposits build up to repair the bone, but the mineralization only makes up for the strength that was lost. Over time, this strength normalizes, and the bone is not more or less likely to break in that same spot. I used to think it was such a nice idea that we gain the most strength in the places that hurt the most, but perhaps the reality of the situation is the better metaphor, after all. Perhaps we can return to normalcy someday—with a few scars and marks. Yet recovery doesn't actually shield us from the wounds to come. Losing Neilia and Naomi couldn't protect Joe from the pain of losing Beau to cancer four decades later.

Maybe the strength we gain is simply the knowledge that survival is possible. Maybe it's the realization that pain isn't fatal, that it allows you to go back out into the world, breakable bones and all.

And maybe being a parent isn't about having answers—instead, it's just continuing on this path of life alongside your children, loving them in your best, flawed way.

Since Beau's death, I'm definitely shattered. I feel like a piece of china that's been glued back together again. The cracks may be imperceptible—but they're there. Look closely, and you can see the glue holding me together, the precarious edges that vein through my heart. I am not the same. I feel it every day. I think every mother who has lost a child must feel this way.

Am I able to feel happiness? Yes, definitely. But it's not as pure; there's just not the magic to life that I used to feel. You'd think after all this time, I might have learned something about survival from a man—from a father—who couldn't be taken down. But here I sit, waiting for healing I fear might never come. Joe promises me it will.

———————

Twenty years after the '88 election and Joe's aneurysm, we had another campaign and another illness.

I took after my father in a lot of ways—I had his eyes, his bone structure, and his temper, as I've mentioned. But my mother was all I wanted to be. She had deep, dark eyes, and auburn hair with soft curls, which she wore in a practical bob. She never had the time for things like makeup or fashionable clothing, but she was funny and quick to laugh. When Halloween rolled around each year, she'd get us dressed from her box of homemade costumes, pour some cocktails, and she and my dad would follow us around the neighborhood, martinis in hand. She was difficult to shock and gave great advice. "Jill," she told me when a high school rival of mine suspiciously invited me to her house, "always fight your battles on your own turf." She was petite but seemed to be impossibly strong—dependable, calm, unflappable in the face of crisis or catastrophe.

It was agony to see that taken from her.

It began with stomach discomfort a few years prior, and she was diagnosed with cancer. Her doctor told her they'd have to remove 85 percent of her stomach. After the surgery, and over the next week in the hospital, her pain didn't seem to be getting any better. She was in the ICU for a while, and even after getting out, she was so sick she couldn't sit up in bed. I drove up to Pennsylvania to see her almost every day, and as I watched her grip the side rail of the bed in pain, I said to my father, "Dad, this isn't right. Something's really wrong with Mom."

"I think so, too," he said.

So I went down to the doctor's office and insisted he come

and have another look. When the doctor saw how much pain she was in, he decided to operate again to find the source.

As it turned out, he had accidentally twisted my mother's bowel while putting it back in—causing her excruciating pain. But we soon learned an even worse truth: she'd never had cancer at all.

The hospital had mistakenly switched my mother's pathology with that of another patient—a woman who did have cancer. The surgeries, the constant pain, all of it a clerical error.

After her surgeries, my hearty, funny, tenacious mother began to fade into a shadow of herself. She could eat only meals the size of her fist and grew thin and frail. I could barely recognize her as the woman I'd known my whole life. And then she did get cancer—lymphoma—and deteriorated even further through the chemo treatments. As her body weakened, dementia came to steal away the rest of the woman we knew.

Her final days came when I was on the campaign trail in 2008. I'd go speak at one event, rush home to sleep, then wake early to drive to Willow Grove so I could see her. I'd stay a couple of hours or a day or two and then head right back out on the road. I worried about her constantly, during speeches in Iowa and while shaking hands on rope lines in the Midwest, calling whenever I could to check in and see how she was.

I played the parent now, always concerned: Is she wearing her warm socks today? Did she see the nurse? Is she comfortable?

There is something terrible about watching someone you love lose independence. Joe and I had always felt that when our parents got older, we wanted them to be able to move in with us—and it was very gratifying when we were able to make that happen. We'd specifically built the Wilmington house to have a big bedroom downstairs—big enough to fit a hospital bed. Dada stayed there for a while, and then, after he died in 2002, we sold Mom Mom's house and put that money into renovating the garage into an in-law apartment.

With Dada, our home became somewhat of a hospice at the end of his life. For seven months, we cared for him and watched over him, all while family members and medical professionals were in and out of our house all day long. It was a lot of work to keep up with his needs, but I had watched my parents care for my grandparents, and I knew it was my responsibility. Family takes care of family. And there was joy in it, too.

The Christmas Eve when Dada was with us, his health was stable, but he wasn't healthy enough to go to late-night Mass, so the two of us stayed home while the rest of the family went to church. His doctors had told him he wasn't allowed to drink, but he had always loved a good glass of wine. Knowing he had so little time left with us, it seemed silly to deny him that small boon, so I broke out a nice bottle, and we sipped our glasses by the fire, our own little Christmas communion.

As difficult as caring for our parents was at times, it also felt like a blessing. Changing feeding tubes, changing clothes, helping them go to the bathroom—I wanted to be the one to help with things so intimate, not a stranger. Our parents had loved us in our helplessness long ago, and here we were, able to return that generosity.

But the worst part of watching my mother slip away wasn't the physical indignities; it was the loss of her as my confidante, my cheerleader. No matter how much I called or how often I visited, I couldn't tell her the things I wanted to. I couldn't make her laugh with my crazy campaign stories. I couldn't complain about whatever silly thing was irking me that day. I couldn't get her advice. I wanted to share my life with her, like I'd always done. I wanted her to be *her*. But so much of her was gone.

Instead, I spoke softly and kissed her on the head. I held her hand and read to her. I held back tears on the long trips to whatever city was next on the docket.

Leading up to the weekend Mom died, I had been up in Willow Grove a lot but had to return home to Wilmington because Beau was leaving for Iraq. He'd joined the National Guard in 2003, and though he'd believed he wouldn't be sent to fight in the Middle East, his unit had been called up. He was serving as the attorney general of Delaware at the time and probably could have gotten a deferment, but he wouldn't hear of it. He decided to deploy with the 261st.

Caught between two realities I didn't want to think about—losing my mother and my son leaving for war—I turned to the only thing that kept me sane: running. I ran as many miles as I could per week, and with all the stress, I had a hard time eating as well. So, over a period of a few months, I lost ten pounds—a lot for me. And while everyone was worried, and I knew I needed to keep up my strength, I just couldn't swallow food. Ashley began mothering me, trying to get me to eat. "Mom," she'd say, "you know I'm always going to be honest with you. People are afraid something's wrong with you." I wanted to go back to my normal routine, but I just couldn't do it.

I was running in Brandywine State Park when a Secret Service car pulled up beside me. An agent rolled down the window and said, "Your mother has taken a turn for the worse. I think you need to call home." Over those months, the men and women of the Secret Service had felt like guardian angels, driving me back and forth at all hours of the day and night, going out of their way to be kind, to be as invisible as possible. As we made the trip to Willow Grove, to my childhood home, I prayed over and over that my mother wouldn't die before I got there.

All of my sisters and I got into my mom's bed and held her. We talked to her; we told stories of our childhood; we laughed and cried. She was surrounded by love. She wasn't fully conscious, but I believe she knew we were there. We didn't sleep that night; we stayed right there in the bed until she died the next morning. It was so hard to let her go—emotionally, physically, spiritually. She left before I was done needing her.

In one emotionally racked week, my mother was gone, my son was a world away, and my husband was out there somewhere, stretched thin on the campaign trail. But Mom always showed me how important it is to be a source of strength for those you love. I asked myself, as I would again and again when faced with a difficult situation, what would she do? And I knew the answer: I packed my suitcase, called my team, and got back on the campaign trail.

I soldiered on, I smiled at events, but for a long time, it felt like a part of me was missing. And once again, when I needed her most, Mom Mom was there. She called often. She came to see me. She made sure I knew I wasn't alone.

For the next few years, when I wanted to call my mother to complain or brag or celebrate, I'd call Mom Mom instead. All the secrets I would only share with my mom now belonged to her. She listened and laughed and gave me advice. I wonder if she knew how much that meant to me. I wonder if she knew that she saved me all those times. I think she probably did. After all, Mom Mom knew just about everything.

11

SMALL WONDERS

Imagine for a moment that you're a White House staffer. There's no such thing as a forty-hour workweek—you're on call all the time. The stakes for almost every project you undertake—from hosting a state dinner, to crafting a policy, to celebrating a milestone—feel, and often are, matters of global importance. It's a job with incredibly fulfilling rewards—pride, honor, and the ability to say you've served our great nation—but the days are long and the level of stress you carry can be so heavy as to be detrimental to your health. If you're not careful, it can grind you down. The White House is a serious place, with serious people, doing serious work.

And that's why, one afternoon during our first term, when we were scheduled to fly to California for an event, I decided to play a little prank. I had arrived at Joint Base Andrews early, coming straight from teaching my classes, and was the first one there. As I boarded Air Force Two, I looked around and had an idea.

The overhead bins were small, but I knew if I scrunched up enough, I could cram myself into one. I climbed up on one of the chairs, stepped onto the table, and then pulled myself into the bin—finally, my ballet barre classes were paying off. One of our naval aides, Tom McNulty, was right behind me, and he was happy to give me a final boost up and pull the door down for me to hold with my fingertips.

When the first person opened the bin to stow his roller bag, I popped halfway out and screamed, "Boo!"—though it was hard to get it out through my laughter. Still, my surprise had the intended effect: this poor soul let out a high-pitched shriek and stumbled backward into his seat, a look of utter shock on his face. The others burst out laughing as I very ungracefully tumbled the rest of the way out of the bin. For the rest of the five-hour flight, the staff genially joked at his expense and mine, recounting the look on his face and how absurd I was to climb up there in the first place.

When I was growing up, pranks were a big part of our family. April Fools' Day was one of our favorite holidays and remains one of mine to this day. I used to tell the kids that school was canceled because of snow, and wait until they stopped cheering and jumping around to break the news with a chipper, "April Fools!" Another time, I screamed to Joe that I'd broken my leg until he came running, terrified, to help me. Poor Joe never seems to remember when it's April 1. Every once in a while, he'll try to pull one over on me, but I'm always on guard, so it never works. What can I say? I learned from the master.

My father was a legend in our neighborhood. He always managed to find the prank we weren't expecting. One year, he set all the clocks back an hour, making us late to things, though that was not as confusing as when he set them forward and we were an hour early. Another year, he mowed our neighbor's lawn in perfectly alternating stripes. He always had a new trick up his sleeve for his girls. But it wasn't just April Fools' Day—he knew how to get us year round. He stuck his finger in every birthday cake, just to goad us. When a new boy showed up for a date, Dad would turn a chair to the wall and make him sit there awkwardly while he waited for one of us. But the worst was when we'd get home from dates. We'd pull up in our boy-friends' cars, nervously making small talk to extend the night or shyly flirting one last time. The excitement of young love and the romance of new possibilities with a handsome boy vibrated in the air—until it was abruptly interrupted by my father play-ing taps on his bugle in the driveway.

I've always believed you've got to steal the joyful moments when you can. Life is difficult, and if you sit around waiting for fun to show up, you'll find yourself going without it more often than not. If I can make Joe laugh by something as silly as hiding under the bed and popping out when the lights are off, why not?

To me, a big part of creating joyful moments comes from surprises; I love them in all their forms. In February of 2009, just a month after the start of the Obama-Biden administration, I decided to surprise Joe for Valentine's Day. But doing that, I realized, would be a lot trickier than in years past. Now that I was Second Lady, it was just about impossible to get around inconspicuously.

We had recently moved into the official vice presidential res-idence in Washington, D.C., and I was still getting used to the particulars of this new life. On the grounds of the U.S. Naval Observatory, the residence was a far cry from our house in Del-aware. It was beautiful, but it was also a bit like moving into a museum. Like all vice presidential families, we were assigned military aides who helped out with the house and a Secret

Service detail who accompanied us everywhere. It was strange to have so many people—as kind and helpful as they were—around all the time. If Joe and I had a disagreement, we didn't feel comfortable hashing it out publicly, so we found other ways to do it. Sometimes, we'd fight by text message, even when we were right there in the same room. We called it "fexting."

Suddenly, I was no longer allowed to drive myself; the Secret Service was always present, ready to take me wherever I needed to go. It might sound nice to have a luxury SUV with a driver—and it was nice!—but sometimes I just wanted the freedom that came from running to the grocery store on a whim. So, on the cold morning before Valentine's Day, I decided to jog the two and a half miles to the White House. I wouldn't be alone, of course, as Secret Service agents would trail behind me in the SUV, but at least I had a little space.

Not only had I not told Joe I was coming, I hadn't told anyone on my staff either. When I got to the White House grounds, I jogged past the pack of reporters and cameras that was always camped out on the driveway, and everyone's phones started buzzing. I guess this wasn't something that Second Ladies often did—and as my team informed me later, they weren't keen on possibly having press photos of me in my spandex beamed around the world.

Once inside the White House grounds, I went to the Secret Service vehicle and took out my tools: half a dozen tubes of paint, all different colors. I headed into the West Wing, and with the help of Joe's longtime, trusted executive assistant, Michele Smith, I sneaked into Joe's office while he was out at a meeting. I then proceeded to paint big multicolored hearts all over his windows for Valentine's Day. When he walked into the office—accompanied by a senator—later that morning, I wasn't there to see his reaction, but I know he was both delighted and embarrassed.

I'm not the most publicly affectionate wife in the world, but Valentine's Day gives me an excuse to go all out. One year, I bought a small boulder from a rock quarry, then had it carved with a heart and our initials, JB + JB. I had it delivered to our front lawn, right beside the driveway of our Delaware home, so Joe would see it when he came home after work. Another year, I carved our initials into one of the big trees in our backyard and hooked up a spotlight to illuminate it. That night it snowed, so when Joe came home, he saw the tree all lit up with snowflakes falling gently around it. It was like something out of a storybook, and Joe's face was one of childlike delight as he stood and looked out at our tree.

Not every plan turns out quite so magically. One year, I put white lights around our canopy bed and scattered rose petals all over it, attempting to channel my most romantic side. Our grandkids came over before Joe got home, and they immediately scooted upstairs to discover my tableau. "Nana!" they shouted. "This is so cool!" They were in grade school, and luckily still associated Valentine's Day with only obligatory punch-out cards, but I was still embarrassed. So much for romance.

Marriage—and life, for that matter—isn't easy. We all get stuck in our routines and find ourselves bogged down by the everyday. If you're not careful, you can go for days passing your spouse in the hall, or drinking coffee at the table together, and failing to look up and really see each other. After more than forty years together, I make a point to try to create extraordinary moments with Joe from time to time. It's one of the best lessons I learned from watching my parents. There's a beautiful poem called "Don't Hesitate" by Mary Oliver that always reminds me to be grateful for the time we have:

> If you suddenly and unexpectedly feel joy,
> don't hesitate. Give in to it. There are plenty
> of lives and whole towns destroyed or about
> to be. We are not wise, and not very often
> kind. And much can never be redeemed.
> Still, life has some possibility left. Perhaps this
> is its way of fighting back, that sometimes
> something happens better than all the riches
> or power in the world. It could be anything,
> but very likely you notice it in the instant
> when love begins. Anyway, that's often the
> case. Anyway, whatever it is, don't be afraid
> of its plenty. Joy is not made to be a crumb.

On a Sunday morning in 2004, our house was struck by lightning and caught fire.

Joe was scheduled to appear on *Meet the Press*, so the network had sent a car to pick him up very early—around 6:00 a.m. Ashley, Hunter, and Beau were all grown and out of the house, so it was just me and our cat, Daisy. I slept in that morning, and when I awoke, a storm had rolled in, and the rain was pounding down. As I walked down the stairs to the kitchen to get some coffee, I heard a tremendous *boom*. It was so loud and so close that I assumed lightning must have struck one of the trees just outside the house.

I started walking around the first floor, looking out the windows to see which tree had been hit, but all of them looked fine. I began to wonder if I'd been mistaken about the lightning strike—but as I walked back into the kitchen, it was filling up with smoke. We kept a fire extinguisher in the cabinet, and I grabbed it, hoping to put out the fire before the whole house went up. But no matter where I looked, I couldn't find the flames. All around me was black smoke, billowing, seemingly coming from the vents in the ceiling—and I realized with horror that the fire had to be *inside* the walls.

Within minutes, the kitchen was so thick with smoke, I couldn't see anything. I grabbed the phone to call 911, but it was dead. I'd been so focused on dealing with the fire, it took me a moment to realize that *I had to get out of the house.* Suddenly terrified, I ran outside, rushed to the closest neighbor's home, and started pounding on their door.

After calling 911 from the neighbor's phone, the next number I dialed was Beau's, since he was living just a couple of miles away. Joe was on the *Meet the Press* set at that very moment, being interviewed by Tim Russert, so there was no point in trying to get in touch with him. It would have to be a terrible surprise whenever he was done.

Suddenly, I realized Daisy was probably still inside the house, curled up on our bed asleep. I ran back up the driveway, threw open the front door, and yelled, "Daisy! *Daisy!*" The smoke was too thick to go in, and I had to shut the door to take a deep breath before trying again. I opened it a second time and screamed again for Daisy, but there was still no sign of her. The third time—just when I felt I wouldn't be able to stand the smoke at the door again—she came roaring down the steps, shot out the door, and disappeared into the woods. We wouldn't be able to find her for three days.

After Daisy escaped, I stood watching the smoke roil out of my house—out every window, every chimney, every doorway. Soon, sirens came blaring down our street, and half a dozen fire engines tore down our driveway and screeched to a halt. The firefighters raced through the front door, and just as quickly they raced back out, the smoke too thick to see anything. They hurried to put on masks and headlamps, and with axes in hands, they rushed back into the house.

The rain was pouring down as I stood in the driveway, watching our home be consumed by flames. I started to shiver from shock and the chilly rain, and a member of the Delaware Women's Auxiliary, which comes to assist in these types of emergency situations, rushed over and handed me a yellow slicker. "Here, put this on," she said. "You've got to cover yourself." It was only then that I realized I was still wearing the thin bathrobe I'd thrown on when I'd awakened.

As I stood there shaking, Beau came running down our driveway. "Mom! Mom!" he shouted, his face white with fear. "Are you okay?" I assured him I was fine, and we hugged each other tightly. Then we watched helplessly, arms around each other, as our beloved house burned.

Suddenly, a firefighter came toward me, calling, "Mrs. Biden!" I looked at him, dreading what was to come. What else could go wrong? What else could we lose today? "Do you remember me?" he asked. "It's Harry!" A giant smile spread across his face. He had been one of my students at Delaware Technical Community College.

"Yeah, Harry," I said, standing there in my drenched bathrobe and yellow slicker. "I *do* remember you." He was a funny, sweet kid who'd taken my class twice. For a brief moment, I laughed at the absurdity of this reunion and felt a tinge of pride that he'd gone on to follow his dream of becoming a firefighter.

When Joe arrived a couple of hours later, the police escorted him down our driveway. I ran up to him. "Oh my God, Joe—look at our house! What are we going to do?" I was soaking wet, emotionally devastated by the damage the fire had done to our home, and already dreading the endless rebuilding process to come.

But Joe just broke into a smile and said, "Look at it this way. Now we can fix all the things we didn't like when it was built!" It was classic Joe: always looking for the silver lining. Even with the house burning—the house I knew he loved more than any of us did—he was the Tigger to my Eeyore. And over the next six months, we did exactly that, making the house not only whole again but also better than it had been before.

One year after the fire, with the house restored *and* improved, our family gathered there for Sunday dinner. We'd started this tradition after the kids moved out, modeling it after those long-ago Sunday dinners of my childhood. As a girl, I enjoyed those dinners, but I couldn't have known how much they must have meant to my grandparents. Now that my kids were out of the house, and I had grandchildren of my own, I understood completely.

Everyone in the family was welcome for Sunday supper, and people usually started showing up around two or three in the afternoon. Mom Mom and Dada would be there, and Ashley, and

Beau and Hunt and their wives, Hallie and Kathleen. Eventually, we had grandkids running around—Hunter's three daughters, Naomi, Finnegan, and Maisy, and Beau's kids, Natalie and little Hunter.

Our house is on a lake, so the water has always been a big part of our lives. The kids particularly loved coming over to use our kayaks, our canoe, and, of course, the swimming pool. For a while, we had a white plastic boat with a little motor, but that one sank. And one year, we gave Joe a dark green rowboat that he named the *Naomi*. Beau loved to fish, and he taught little Hunter how to fish as well—the two of them would sit with their poles on the dock, catch a few fish, and then toss them back in the water. The weathered old dock always had rubber fishing lures scattered around, and a couple of beat-up Adirondack chairs.

The kids would spend the afternoon on the dock or in the boats, rowing to the little island out in the middle of the pond. The girls would sit around the pool, just relaxing, sunning, and reading, and the grown-ups would sit on the patio, chatting about whatever story was in the Sunday *New York Times* or Wilmington's *News Journal*. It was an almost perfect scene, with woods all around, kids playing and splashing, geese on the pond (and thus goose poop all over the yard). Eventually, the little ones would splash around in the pool, playing Marco Polo. I loved seeing them having fun, though that was the one game that always drove me crazy, with the shouts of "Marco!" and "Polo!" constantly piercing the air. It was the kind of annoyance I would miss terribly when they were gone.

In the morning, I'd go to Haskell's local farm market to pick up summer corn, tomatoes, peaches, and basil. We'd make a big salad, and everyone would bring something to pitch in. Sunday dinner meant grilled chicken breasts, salads, and pasta for Joe because he *always* wants pasta. I'd make a pie for Dada—peach, his favorite. Sometimes we'd get bushels of crabs, and everyone would bang away with the wooden mallets on newspapers, the smell of Old Bay seasoning on our hands and clothes. The dogs—German shepherds, rescue dogs, labradoodles—would sleep all over each other or attempt to steal a bite from the table.

And that's how we spent every Sunday, for years. Not everyone came every week—sometimes it would be Hunter and his family, sometimes Beau and his. For a while, both were living in Wilmington, but when Hunter and his family moved to Washington, D.C., it wasn't as easy for them to come up. I cherished the days when everyone was there, when their busy lives aligned in the right way and allowed them all to join us.

Mom Mom never missed a Sunday dinner. She'd come sit by the pool and have a glass of Coca-Cola, and we'd set out trays of chips and pretzels like a cocktail hour. The grandkids adored Mom Mom—everyone wanted to sit next to her, hear her stories, and look after her.

Sunday dinners were one of our most meaningful traditions, and while they were less practical when we joined the administration, we tried to keep at least some of our dinner traditions alive. Like all vice presidential families, we were assigned naval enlisted aides (called NEAs) who helped out at our official D.C. residence and did most of the cooking. I had no complaints, as they were wonderful cooks, and it was hugely helpful to have people there to support us, but, as a result, hosting big, easy-going family gatherings could be complicated. I wanted to be respectful of our NEAs' work and time, so when the family did get together, I often tried to take on the job of cooking, to varying degrees of success.

The first year we were at the Vice President's Residence, I was set on making Hunter's birthday chicken potpie. I made it every alternate year, after all, and that tradition didn't have to end just because we had a new house. Sure, the residence had an industrial kitchen rather than a normal-size one, but a kitchen was a kitchen, right?

My first sign of trouble was that there were no mixing bowls, or at least none I could find that were not the size of barrels. The basic ingredients, including salt, stock, and chicken, were all stored by what appeared to be the metric ton. Simply getting a cup of flour was an ordeal. The industrial ovens cooked differently from my average-size one at home, and I needed an instruction guide just to turn on the range. Wandering around the sprawling room, searching in vain for a measuring spoon, I felt like Lucy Ricardo. The result was a bit of a mess.

For Ashley's birthday, I aimed much lower, making sure we had the ice cream cake she always liked. *At least you can't mess up a store-bought cake,* I thought as I slipped it into the freezer. It was only later, when we pulled out a box of soggy cream, that I realized the freezer it was in, a steel closet in a wall full of steel closets, was not actually the freezer but yet another fridge.

Luckily for me, Hunter and Ashley saw the humor in those situations. And while my culinary disasters weren't meals that anyone would want to eat again, they were unforgettable. We laughed together as we spooned soupy bites of melted ice cream into our mouths. Those were some of the many times I was grateful my family didn't take themselves too seriously.

The traditions that have really stuck with us are the ones that reflect what we're about as a family: togetherness and generosity toward one another. And the routines around these traditions remind us of our history—no matter what we had for the meal, I'd always set the table, adding flowers and lighting candles just as my mother had, to bring little touches of beauty.

In some ways, our dinners weren't anything special—they were casual afternoons together with homemade food. But that was exactly what made them perfect—that, and the laughter and love and gratitude for each other. Not a crumb of joy, but a feast. As the novelist Barbara Kingsolver once wrote, "Maybe life doesn't get any better than this, or any worse, and what we get is just what we're willing to find: small wonders, where they grow."

12

DECISIONS TOGETHER

The moment that young Beau and Hunter told their dad that "we should marry Jill," the boys established an unofficial protocol for almost all of the major Biden questions. When decisions affected us all, we all had a say in the decision-making process. For something as important as the boys taking on a new mother, it was only fair. But over time, I've come to appreciate this tradition as part of what keeps our family close. I am an introverted community college teacher married to an extroverted U.S. senator, and Joe always understood that a public life was his choice, not mine. It may be his name on the ticket, but all of us—me, the kids, and now the grandkids—have to talk to reporters, show up at rallies, and deal with the scrutiny. So we decide together. And because we all have a say, we all have a role to play when the choice is made.

For years, I was apprehensive about the idea of another presidential run, but that didn't stop people from occasionally trying to persuade Joe. And so, despite the fact that I had forbidden any campaign talk, a group of party leaders came to our house in 2003 to make the pitch. They sat themselves down in our living room and spoke to Joe for hours about how he was the only one who could take on President Bush.

Meanwhile, I was sitting at the pool in my swimsuit, fuming. We had already decided that we weren't running, but people kept insisting on having these meetings with him. So, as party advisors gamed out their strategy for a theoretical run for president, my temper got the best of me. I decided I needed to contribute to this conversation. As I walked through the kitchen, a Sharpie caught my eye. I drew *NO* on my stomach in big letters, and marched through the room in my bikini.

Needless to say, they got the message.

However, four years later, for the election in 2008, things were different. By then, we were years into two wars that didn't seem to have an end. I watched as our troops were asked to give more and more, while their families back home had to make do through multiple deployments. With Beau in the National Guard, I was fearful he'd be called to serve, and I felt closer and closer to the families who were carrying so much of the burden for our national security.

Joe had spent years on the Foreign Relations Committee; as a result, he had been to Afghanistan and Iraq a number of times and had built relationships with leaders there. Over decades in the Senate, he had become a trusted statesman, working for America's interests as well as for the good of struggling people around the world. To my mind, Joe had the most experience, insight, and levelheaded expertise to navigate us away from disaster in Iraq and Afghanistan.

So I organized a family meeting to suggest he—and by extension, we—do it. I asked all of the kids to come over—Hunter drove up from D.C. and Ashley from Philly, while Beau came from across town. It was a Saturday afternoon, and we met in the library of our home. Joe thought the kids had just decided to come for dinner, so when he walked into the library to find all of us staring intently at him, he had no idea what to expect. He looked a little bewildered as he realized this was an ambush. I stood up to drive home my point. "Joe," I said, "it's time. You have to run." He listened quietly as each of us made our case— Beau itching to get on the campaign trail, Hunter adamant that the nation needed a man like Joe, Ashley excited by the prospect of what we could do together. Uncharacteristically, Joe didn't say much, but I could tell he was grateful for our enthusiasm. So it was decided.

For several months, our whole family—grandkids and in-laws included—campaigned. Everyone would pile into a van and drive hours and hours to events all over the country—with the grandkids telling people in Iowa and New Hampshire about how fantastic their pop was. We even gave up Nantucket to spend the Thanksgiving holiday at a tiny French restaurant in Des Moines, Iowa, on the campaign trail. And while we were out there, I could see exactly how we might improve the growing problems in our country. Joe gave it everything he had, and I was proud of him. But in the end, it wasn't his year, and we had little choice but to end the campaign in January.

I knew that if Joe were president, he would work hard for the men and women serving our nation, as well as their families back home. But flying home from the announcement in Iowa, realizing a presidential bid was no longer on the table, I had to find another way to get involved, so I called the National Guard in Delaware and asked how I could help. They put me in touch with a new group, formed by five women who were mothers and spouses of Guardsmen, called Delaware Boots on the Ground (DBOTG).

DBOTG provides services for military families in need. If a spouse is deployed and the family's heating system breaks, DBOTG takes care of the problem. If someone needs his car repaired or help with her pets or any of a million other things, we would get it done. Once, we got a call after a young mother, unable to cope alone while her spouse was deployed, had dropped off her baby at the grandmother's house. The grandma didn't have any of the things she needed to care for an infant—no diapers, no crib, nothing—so DBOTG ordered everything she needed and had it delivered the next day.

As I saw again and again, the decision to join the military affects a person's entire family in ways big and small, anticipated and unanticipated. And it is a decision that is so often fraught with the push-pull that comes from choosing a path of honor that requires service members to leave their loved ones behind.

When I was a little girl, my father used to take us to a park in his hometown, Hammonton, New Jersey, to visit the World War II monument. It was a modest stone obelisk with the names in bronze of the local men who fought—including his own. I know my grandmother was upset when my dad enlisted in World War II, but ultimately, she signed papers to allow him to join at the age of just seventeen.

Moved by 9/11, Beau was commissioned in the National Guard in 2003. It happened fast—Joe was the one who actually told me, on the morning of Beau's enlistment ceremony. I was nothing but proud that he chose to follow in his grandfather's footsteps and serve our country—but as the Iraq war was just getting started, I was blindsided by his decision. I was worried he would be deployed to one of the most dangerous places in the world and terrified he wouldn't come home.

My feelings were a complicated mixture of fear and pride, something I think is probably true of most Blue Star Families. Still, Beau was in his thirties and didn't need to ask for my permission. A sense of duty was one of the values we had instilled in him, and I didn't get to decide how that manifested in his life, so like my Grandmom Jacobs supported my father, I supported Beau.

Over the years, I've met his brothers and sisters in arms, and I've seen how deeply that sense of duty runs through our troops. My admiration for their service and sacrifice has only grown. But through DBOTG, I saw another side of that coin—I saw more clearly how the families of our military serve in their own way. At deployment and homecoming ceremonies, I saw the bookending emotions of sorrow and sheer joy as families were separated from each other and brought back together again. I watched kids, barely old enough for school, put on a brave face as they admitted they were torn between missing their dad or mom desperately and feeling pride that their parents were helping. I saw spouses struggling to balance the checkbook, organize day care, find jobs, and step in while their partner was halfway across the world. I saw how much they all sacrificed in order to keep us safe.

After Joe's 2008 campaign ended, I was glad to have DBOTG to work on. I found purpose in supporting these families during times of such upheaval, especially as my own family settled back into our normal life.

Still in the Senate, Joe was commuting to D.C. every day, I

was working at Del Tech, and the kids were focusing on their own careers. Things were familiar: I'd wake up early in the morning to go for a run. I'd enjoy a hot cup of coffee afterward and make some toast—maybe bring a slice to Joe—then grab my schoolbag and head across town to class. At night, we'd catch up over dinner, tell stories about our days' events, and talk about what new adventures the kids were pursuing.

Of course, we'd watch some of the campaign coverage, and even though the loss was difficult, it was exciting to see the election play out. We knew we were witnessing history being made, as either the first woman or the first African American was about to be nominated as a presidential candidate by a major political party.

One afternoon in June, I was driving home from an event in Dover with Delaware governor Ruth Ann Minner. She had declared the week of July 4 a week of the military, so we were traveling the state to support businesses and nonprofits that were giving to military causes. We were almost home to Wilmington when Joe called me on my cell phone. "Barack asked if I would agree to be vetted to be vice president. He said I should discuss it with the family," he told me.

"Oh my God, okay," I said. This was out of left field—the possibility of vice president hadn't entered my mind. "What time will you be home?" I asked. "I'll call the kids so we can get together and talk about it." As Barack had anticipated, this would be a family decision.

Joe had been in the Senate for most of his working life, a place where he was his own boss. He loved everything about the Senate, from the committees he was on, to the day-to-day work, to the people—and everyone from his staff, to the interns, to the people who run the elevators. And they loved him, too, consistently voting him the most-liked senator. Joe truly enjoyed going to work because being a senator played to his strengths and because he was able to make a real difference in people's lives. So leaving that job, even for one as incredible as the vice presidency, was a big decision.

The rest of the family was less hesitant. Hunter, Ashley, Beau, and I all thought that if the job was offered, it would be the chance of a lifetime. I knew Joe's experience would be invaluable and that he could help usher in the leadership our country needed. I believed he could do a lot of good as vice president, and it would be an amazing adventure for our family.

Joe didn't make a decision that day, but the next day he called in more of the family to get their opinions. Even Mom Mom spoke up. "You've always fought so hard for civil rights, honey—it's a big part of who you are. Don't you want to be a part of this history?" she asked. The kids kept calling me throughout the day, giving me advice on what to say to move the decision along. Joe loved being a senator, but at the same time he understood the importance and relevance of this historic ticket.

That night he told Barack that yes, we would agree to be vetted.

Everything was kept secret so that word of who was being considered wouldn't leak. But when David Axelrod and David Plouffe flew up to Wilmington to interview Joe, I decided we should pick them up ourselves rather than sending a staff member, to give them a sense of how our family operates. I called

Beau and asked if he'd come with me, and the two of us picked up the Davids and chatted with them all the way to Val's house, which was where the interview took place. The Bidens are a team, and on this visit, Barack's advisors would see that up close.

Even as our family had entered into the vetting process, we heard rumors of the other impressive names on the list, and we were cautious in our optimism that Joe would actually be chosen. Any time my mind started to wander toward thoughts of the White House, I stopped it short. There was no need to get our hopes up.

But by mid-August, things had begun to change. Word was out that Joe was on the short list, and a pack of reporters had camped themselves at the top of our driveway in anticipation. I had planted some beautiful red-and-white impatiens there, and they were quickly trampled all to hell. Every time we tried to leave the house, we were met by questions and camera flashes. The phone rang off the hook with interview requests. In fact, I became so overwhelmed with it one night that I convinced Joe to sneak out the back door and go through the neighbor's yard, where we slunk through the bushes and waited for Beau to pick us up. He drove us away from the frenzy, and we were able to take a quiet walk around the dark neighborhood, finally getting some peace.

Joe got the call on a Thursday when he was sitting in the waiting room of our dentist's office. I was back at school at that point, so he had picked me up after my classes were over to take me to have a root canal. I would be drowsy after the surgery, and he wasn't about to let me drive home. So there in the waiting room, probably while he mindlessly flipped through the latest issue of *Time* or *Architectural Digest*, his phone alerted him that Barack Obama was calling.

That afternoon, as the dentist had been drilling into my tooth, the decision had been finalized. As soon as I was out of the chair, with my head drowsy and my jaw sore, Joe quickly ushered me to the car. "Barack asked me to be his running mate," he blurted as soon as the doors were shut.

"I'm so proud of you, Joe!" I tried to say. But with my lips still numb, all I could muster was a jumbled mess of half words and a crooked smile.

We were still in bed the next morning when we saw the first news helicopter through our open bedroom window. I rushed out of bed, clutching a blanket around my pajamas—not a look I was hoping to showcase on the news—and yanked the curtains closed. We were just hours away from the text message that would name Joe as vice presidential candidate to the Obama team's millions of subscribers, and our home was filling up with Secret Service, strategists, and friends who would help us get ready for the coming weeks. Campaign staff whisked us off to Springfield, Illinois, for the announcement that afternoon, and a private plane returned us that night. It was such a whirlwind, I didn't even have time to buy an appropriate outfit and had to borrow a suit from my sister-in-law Sara.

Sunday morning, bright and early, a pile of red, white, and blue dresses as tall as I was showed up on our doorstep. I spent the next few hours with my new trip director, Carrie Devine, changing in and out of clothes. "Well, I certainly didn't expect to be spending the day getting dressed and undressed with someone I just met," I joked to her.

We officially hit the campaign trail on Monday—beginning

with the national convention—and it didn't get any less hectic from there. We had talking points to memorize, policy to learn, and speeches to prepare for. Nothing in our Senate lives was this intense, this enormous, and now the eyes of the nation were on us. Suddenly, *Vogue* magazine was calling, asking to do a feature on the women in Joe's life. It felt surreal: Anna Wintour now had thoughts on my hairstyle, and the famous photographer Arthur Elgort was setting up a camera in my backyard. And of course it wasn't all glamorous. On Delaware's primary day, I jogged to the polls in my running clothes, and my trip coordinator got a terse call from our communications team. "Did she think there wouldn't be cameras?!" they scolded.

On top of all of it, my normal life had to continue. I taught classes Monday through Thursday, so my campaign trips had to be squeezed into the weekends. I still had tests to grade and students to advise. And then there was my mother's health, which was steadily declining following her lymphoma diagnosis.

I was at the convention when I learned she had just weeks to live. We were on our way to a breakfast to greet one of the state delegations, and the Secret Service had just pulled into a parking spot beneath a Denver hotel. I began shaking as I listened to my sister's voice on the other end of the phone, and I couldn't stop the tears that came. Joe held me as the Secret Service stepped out of the car to give us some privacy. All I wanted was to be with my mother at that moment. But I knew it would have to wait.

I gave myself a few minutes to be heartbroken, and then I put those feelings away. My sisters were already rallying together and creating a plan to care for my mother in this final stretch of her life, and I leaned heavily on their support. And for the next few months, I learned to compartmentalize pieces of myself. I wasn't disingenuous when I smiled at rallies or campaign stops; I just had to teach myself to forget for a little while the parts of me that were hurting. The election, the people who came out to support us, the work that went on behind the scenes by so many talented, tireless people—these things were just too important.

Compartmentalizing is a skill you have to learn in politics, and it's one that served me well in our White House years. Still, so many of us, public figures or not, have to learn how to lead these double lives. Work doesn't stop because your father is sick. Deadlines don't go away because your friend is dying. We never know what's behind someone's smile, what hardships they are balancing with their day-to-day responsibilities.

The campaign was a strange world, and though it was exhilarating to be a part of something so remarkable, it was also overwhelming. Operating at this level was more intense than anything I'd done before. For the first time, I wasn't just a surrogate filling in for Joe; I had my own staff, my own travel schedule, even my own charter aircraft. It didn't matter that some of us were naturally reserved or that we had jobs and responsibilities of our own. We had to handle it the Biden way: together.

We all pushed ourselves. We all grew into our roles. And we leaned on each other when we felt frustrated or overwhelmed. When I was exhausted or sad about my mother, I had our family—Beau and Hunt, Ashley and Val, and Joe and Mom Mom—to lean on. My sisters helped take on more responsibilities with my mom's hospice care, and our friends were there, showing up unasked to drop off a platter of chicken salad or basket of fruit. And of course, we now had a new and growing family of amazing staff, thinking of every little thing we could need before we knew we needed it, and Secret Service turning our house into a fortress and driving us wherever we needed to go.

On Election Night, I wanted to temper my hopes for the final result, but I couldn't help being swept away by the excitement. At every stop, every rally, there had been thousands and thousands of people—it took my breath away. I could feel how badly they wanted us to win, I could see how many hopes and dreams were riding on our shoulders. Something big was happening, something incredible and historic—it was palpable.

The day of the election, we started by voting in Delaware that morning, did three last-minute campaign stops, and then ended up in Chicago. Joe lay down for a nap that afternoon, but I was too nervous and excited to be still, so I went for a short walk outside the hotel. I met up with one of my advisors, Cathy Russell—who would become my chief of staff—and we treated ourselves to wine and french fries. When I got back up to our hotel suite, the whole Biden family was there, and the early returns were looking good.

Not long after that, the networks called the race. And in an instant, everything went into motion: phones were ringing, and the Secret Service detail bulked up. It was official—we'd won! I was in the hotel suite getting my hair done when someone came in and said to Joe, "Congratulations, Mr. Vice President. The Obamas are ready for you."

Joe and I went up to the Obamas' suite and found them sitting on a couch—Barack and Michelle; Michelle's mom, Marian

Robinson; and Valerie Jarrett. We hugged each other. We were excited, but the moment was subdued rather than celebratory, almost solemn. We had won—and now there was work ahead.

We rode to Grant Park, where a million people had gathered in anticipation. Arriving at the park with Joe, Hunter, and Ashley, we all felt the absence of Beau, who was in Iraq with his National Guard unit. We couldn't imagine celebrating without him, so we arranged to carry a laptop with us, to Skype with Beau and his unit. When Beau's handsome face appeared on the screen, a part of my heart locked back into place. He smiled as the rest of his unit in Baghdad cheered behind him, all eating pizza and wearing shorts in the desert heat. I felt a surge of pride, and when we walked out onto the stage to the roar of a million voices, we turned the laptop so Beau could see the crowd. In that moment, my family was together again.

Situations may change, we may change, and decisions big and small may need to be made, but one thing stays the same: the Bidens had done this together, as a family.

13

THE TABLE GROWS

Having it all" really means giving it all, doesn't it? It's a quixotic equation—100 percent to our jobs, 100 percent to our families, 100 percent to those parts of us that make us most who we are. But we keep aiming for it because each part of our lives—each part of ourselves—is so important.

Choosing to be a full-time professor as well as Second Lady was challenging. I had to learn to toggle back and forth between the roles and train myself to focus on what was in front of me. I had to be fully present for my students when I was with them, not thinking about event logistics or an upcoming ceremony—and vice versa for my staff meetings at the White House. I had become pretty good at compartmentalizing over the years, but being in the administration took it to a whole new level.

Still, as I juggled my two jobs, I didn't want to shortchange my family role either. My grown children didn't need me making them sandwiches or showing up for hot dog day any longer, but that didn't mean I didn't want to continue being a major part of my children's lives—and, even more critical to me now, my grandchildren's lives. We still hosted big family gatherings, especially for birthdays, but our "free weekends" were a lot harder to come by. Instead, we tried to find ways to integrate the kids into the less flexible obligations we had, whenever it was feasible.

That's how fourteen-year-old Finnegan ended up seated next to me in an armored off-road vehicle, bumping along through the heart of Africa toward the east border of the Democratic Republic of the Congo (DRC).

It was 2014, and we had landed in the city of Bukavu at an airport that wasn't much more than a runway. The DRC is a country rich in natural resources such as oil, minerals, and precious metals, but twenty years of one of the bloodiest tribal-civil wars ever known had made its people some of the poorest in the world. We stepped off the plane and felt the air around us vibrate, as if the ghosts of a generation lost were closing in on us.

On winding red roads that snaked through the hills like battle scars, we were headed to a place I'd heard a lot about over the previous months: Dr. Denis Mukwege's Panzi Hospital. Years before he would become the 2018 Nobel Peace laureate, Dr. Mukwege and his hospital were little known to most Americans. His one mission was to treat women and girls who had been raped by gangs and soldiers. The stories haunted me: women of all ages gruesomely, brutally tortured as an act of war. Often wounded beyond recognition, unable to control their bladders and bowels, these women were turned out of homes and had to walk for days to find refuge at Panzi Hospital.

I had feared a visit to east Congo might be too much for

Finnegan. Was she old enough to process what was going on? She would hear and see a lot of troubling things—from raped women to child soldiers to refugees. Yet this was the real world, and a world we couldn't ignore. She was thoughtful and perceptive beyond her age, and it was important for her to understand the privileges and responsibilities we had as a family in public service and as people who had been lucky enough to be born in this peaceful, wealthy nation. In the end, her parents, Hunter and Kathleen, felt she could handle the trip, and the decision was made: Finnegan would travel with me to Africa.

As we passed the lush green countryside and scattering of homes, I looked at Finnegan and squeezed her hand. I marveled at how she had grown into a bright and curious young woman over the last few years. Still, even as she spoke with such composure to the Secret Service agents who rode in the front seat to safely shepherd us through the country, I could see faint traces in her round face of that little child she had once been. She was old enough for this experience, but it would challenge her. It would challenge me, too. But Joe and I have found that a family grows best if we are willing to change ourselves, accept change in others, and always grow together.

When I became a grandmother, I'll admit I wasn't ready—not for my first grandchild, but for the title. I felt far too young for a word that seemed so old. In my mind, my own grandmothers were so much further along in life than I was—not just in age, but in the kind of grandmotherly perspective I was sure came with the honorific. I had always wanted to be a grandparent like my Grandmom Jacobs: calm, assured, ready with sage advice or a perfectly timed hug. She always seemed to know just what we needed, and she could give a wink and nod that instantly brought confidence: *you've got this*. At forty-two years old, I didn't feel ready to step into her shoes.

But on December 21, 1993, Christmas came early for the Bidens when our first grandchild was born, to Hunter and Kathleen. We were incredibly excited to meet Naomi, named after her father's deceased little sister. Hunter and Kathleen were natural parents—never nervous or worried about how to care for Naomi. I was so proud to see them slide into their roles as if they had always been mom and dad. Roberta, Kathleen's mom, would be "Grandma," so I chose my great-grandmother's moniker, "Nana." And to my surprise, it fit.

Naomi was one of the easiest babies; she was a joy from the moment she was born. Even after being a mother, I wasn't ready for how much I would love that little child. When she was a toddler, my favorite thing was to steal her away for a day or two, just the two of us. I'd go to a friend's place in New Jersey and spend hours on the shore, just watching her crawl around in the sand. I'd forgotten how magical the world looked through a child's eyes, but with Naomi, every shell, every wave, every sandy afternoon had a brand-new sparkle to it.

Finnegan, Hunter and Kathleen's second daughter, came next. She was named Jean Finnegan Biden after Mom Mom. And just like her namesake, she's full of spunk and determination. Third came Roberta Mabel, named after Kathleen's mom and my favorite grandmother, Mabel Jacobs. In a way, she brings together both sides of her family. Children are good for that—bringing the different parts of a family together around a

small, delicate, astonishing person. My grandfather had a nickname for his Mabel, and it seemed to fit our newest little one
perfectly: Maisy.

You become a parent by jumping in feetfirst. You have to
learn as you go. No rehearsal can prepare you for the highs and
lows of parenthood, or how intense the emotions are. People
talk about how it's a love unlike any other—and that's true.
It runs through you like your bloodstream; it's rooted deep in
your cerebellum, like muscle memory you've had your whole
life. But we talk less about how you experience fear unlike any
other as well. How you don't just worry about dangers, you see
them, vividly, in your mind's eye: a tumble down the stairs, a
slip in the street, a piece of food lodged in their tiny throats. And
despite your best intentions, someone breaks a leg or gets a cut
that needs stitches anyway, and you end up feeling guilty that
you didn't protect them. You feel the reverberations of every
mistake you might make before it happens, and then you replay
your missteps for ages. Raising children is magical, but fraught.

However, with Naomi and her sisters, and later Beau and
Hallie's children, Natalie and Hunter, it was all of that intense
love with none of the fear. Despite the boundaries I set with my
own kids—what they could eat, where they could play, when
they had to be in bed—I said yes to everything the grandkids
wanted. Dessert for dinner? Why not! Stay up and hang out
with Nana all night? Of course! I didn't have to tell them to
clean their rooms or worry that wavering on a decision would
spoil them—that was their parents' job. I only ever had to think
about making them happy, and getting the most out of every
single second. It was all of the joys of parenthood without any
of the hard parts.

Joe and my kids have often commented on how much more affectionate I am with the grandkids than anyone else. I don't know what to tell them—it just comes easy. When I'm around my grandchildren, I remember how incredible life can be. To my surprise, I feel younger. And I never want to miss a chance to connect with them in whatever way I can.

When it came to finding a partner, I only ever wanted one thing for my children: someone who loves them as much as they deserve to be loved. Hunter, Beau, and Ashley found that love in Kathleen, Hallie, and Howard. And I, too, love all the people my kids chose to marry. I knew how hard it could be to come into a family like ours, one that was so close, so I always tried to make my children's partners feel like blood relatives, not "in-laws." My parents were my role models for this; they had always supported us but didn't overstep our boundaries. I never wanted to fall into the old stereotype of thinking I alone knew the right way to cook my kids' favorite meals—while, of course, having to catch myself as I wondered why on earth my daughters-in-law didn't fold socks, or execute some other irrelevant task, the exact way I did.

I suddenly had new sympathy for all the times Mom Mom's advice seemed like more than a suggestion. It was difficult to step back and let my children figure out their own way—but Mom Mom had given me the space I needed when I needed it most, and I knew I would have to learn to keep my mouth shut at times as well. I didn't always succeed, and I've been far from a perfect mother to my children's partners, but I hope each of them knows how glad I am that they came into our lives.

A good marriage is founded on compromise, but after my children got married, and especially after they started having children of their own, I learned that compromise goes beyond just the decisions spouses make together. As our table grew, suddenly we were the ones demanding holidays and feeling slighted when we didn't get to see the grandkids. Christmas negotiations were difficult for the first few years that the kids were married. We initially tried a number of permutations, but finally settled on a compromise that worked: we got Christmas Eve and the other parents got Christmas Day.

Our tradition for Christmas Eve is to go to the Children's Mass at St. Joseph's—complete with a visit from Santa—and come home for a huge dinner. I fill up the table with wreaths and twinkling lights and candles, and put a small party gift on every-one's place setting, like a small monogrammed calendar or an ornament. Everyone spends the night—kids piling into the basement and giggling a little too long, parents claiming "their" rooms even though they haven't lived with us in decades.

On Christmas morning, we open presents and I make bacon-egg-and-cheese sandwiches so that everyone has something to eat on their journey to see the other sides of their families. The house always sounds too quiet after everyone leaves, and I usually spend the rest of the day with my sisters. It's a per-fect compromise because we all get some of what we want, but maybe not everything.

Like so many aspects of being a parent, these sacrifices are blessings, too. A part of us wants our children to always need us, always be around, always prefer our sock-folding, or always think we are the most important people in their lives. But we know that would mean they weren't growing or living their fullest lives. Success in parenthood means preparing your children to go out into the world and leave you behind. You try to give your kids everything so that one day they will give their kids everything. I think it's a little bit heartbreaking for parents when they realize they have to take a back seat in the life of someone they love so much, but in the end, it's a small price to pay for their happiness.

I've also realized that, while my kids might not need me as much as they once did, holding our family together, especially for the grandkids, will always be one of my responsibilities. Relationships are complicated, and sometimes, no matter how hard people try, they don't work out. It's terrible to watch people you love struggle in their marriages, and it's especially hard when kids are involved. In the midst of heartbreaks, however, we have all worked to make sure the grandkids feel safe and loved. Our home is open for everyone, whether Naomi wants a place to bring friends for the weekend, or Maisy is looking for a quiet place to study, or little Hunter needs a place to fish.

We've built a lot of traditions over the years, and one of my jobs is to keep them going. In our most turbulent times, they are the scaffolding we cling to. I never realized how vital birthday dinners and Christmas lists could be until they were the only things that seemed to remain unchanged.

I may not feel that I have all of the sage wisdom Grandmom Jacobs seemed to have when she was in this position, but I have learned a lot over my years. I'm not one for lectures or prescriptive lessons, but I do love sharing my passions with my grandkids. I find that the best way I can help guide my grandchildren along their own paths is to be open to learning and possibilities myself.

In the Congo, Finnegan and I were surprised to find that, despite the sorrows that have built Panzi Hospital, it is not a place of mourning. As we drove through the gates, we could feel the air change around us. It's an oasis of love. A place where miracles happen—where women are brought back to life. Dr. Mukwege has a disarming smile and a deep, soothing voice that makes the women he treats feel seen and safe. Walking from room to room, we watched mothers play with their children. Friends gathered, and laughter rang out. In the aftermath of the most inhuman violence imaginable, stripped of their dignity and health, the women of Panzi Hospital created a family, and in that family, they found healing and sanctuary. The depths of their pain had been filled with gratitude for this doctor who had sewn up and patched together their broken lives, and for the new sisters and aunts and grandmothers who had made them whole again.

Walking through the open-air hallways, Finnegan and I heard the strong, hopeful, melodious voices of women and girls surround us. And as we turned the corner, we saw a visual embodiment of endurance, strength, and happiness that would never leave me: a group of women, dressed in vibrant wraps and skirts from every color of the rainbow, singing and dancing to a song of welcome for us. I couldn't understand the words, but I heard the joy in their voices. We later learned that was the name of the rehabilitation center: City of Joy.

Before the trip to the Congo, I told Finnegan that she could step away at any point, that she didn't have to sit through the discussions or tours and listen to all of the heartbreaking details.

But she never took me up on it. She wanted to learn, wanted to stare the truth right in the eyes. A few years later, Panzi Hospital became the subject of one of her school essays. I'm so proud of how she handled herself at that young age, of her unwillingness to look away, and how years later she still recalls the details, and remembers the lesson we both learned that day—about looking at the depths of humanity's worst evils to experience the heights of our compassion, hope, and love.

Joe and I recently took Naomi and Finnegan to see *To Kill a Mockingbird* on Broadway. Afterward, over an Italian dinner at Carmine's—a tradition from their childhood—we talked about all the things that have changed over the years. The girls aren't kids any longer—Naomi is in law school and Finnegan is in college. They are so thoughtful about the world around them. It was wonderful and strange to sit in that dim candlelight and talk to them as adults. Again, I was seeing the world in new ways through their eyes.

This happened recently with little Hunter, as well. Like Beau, little Hunter loves all things military. When it was time to lay the keel for the USS *Delaware*, for which I was honored to be named the sponsor, he was the one I wanted by my side. We saw where the heart of the Virginia-class attack submarine would be laid, and he peppered our guides with thoughtful questions. He looked so much older than ten in his navy suit jacket and tie, and his face beamed as they welded my initials into a piece of steel that would become part of the submarine. He's beginning to have the same mannerisms, the same unassuming strength that defined his dad. I see so much of Beau in him, and I feel like I get a part of my son back when I spend time with Hunt. Whenever I think I'm doing something for him, I end up getting so much more out of it myself.

That's true of all my grandchildren. They give me new eyes for the things I thought I already knew. They surprise me. They remind me of how far we've come and the ceremonies we keep to remember that path. And with them, we create new moments, new traditions. We continue building our family and finding sanctuary in each other. Through them, I feel all the love I've given throughout the years coming back to me.

There are so many things we can't control. There are times we fall short of giving 100 percent to all the obligations in our life. As a parent, as a mother-in-law, as a grandmother, I know I've made mistakes. But each year, as I set the table for Thanksgiving or Christmas Eve, as the number of place settings shrinks or grows, one thing never changes: how deeply grateful I feel for this family, for the moments we have together, for the people who come into our lives—even when they sometimes leave. And when it comes to my grandchildren, I realize how lucky I am to know them, to learn from them, and to love them. I'm so lucky to be Nana.

14

FROM FRIENDS TO FAMILY

Many of the most important people in my life have come to me by surprise. Like with Joe's first phone call, people show up out of the blue—and then, suddenly, they become friends who seem to have known us our entire lives, and we can't imagine what we would do without them.

When we moved to D.C., I knew we would have the chance to do good work. I knew it was an incredible opportunity to make changes for the people in our lives: our neighbors in places like Wilmington and Willow Grove, the students I taught every day, the military families I worked with through DBOTG. But I didn't know we would build friendships that would come to mean so much to us.

The first time I met Michelle Obama was at one of the debates early in the 2007 primary season. All of the candidates' spouses were seated next to each other, and our group was an awkward collection. We greeted each other with tense amicability, as if we all wanted to say, "It's so nice to meet you; I hope your husband does terribly." Still, Michelle was personable and warm, and though we were clearly on different teams, she leaned over and whispered, "I like your shoes."

Michelle had called me to offer congratulations shortly after the decision to add Joe to the ticket was made. Our next face-to-face meeting was in Springfield, when her husband announced Joe as his running mate. I remember that moment so clearly: she wore an A-line shirtdress with purple and gray flowers, the kind of practical yet effortlessly chic look she would come to be known for. Like me, she had a career of her own—the title of First Lady wasn't one she was seeking, but she believed deeply in Barack's leadership and did everything she could to support him. As our husbands spoke on the stage above us, she turned to me and asked, "Jill, have you given any thought to what you'd want to work on if we win?"

"Yes," I told her, thinking of my growing community of National Guard spouses and children. "Military families."

"Me, too!" she replied, and we had an instant connection. As Joe wrapped up his speech to the Illinois crowd, we walked onstage to join our husbands, arm in arm. I had no idea yet that the Obamas would become so much more than running mates, so much more than colleagues, but true friends—and a part of our family.

Walter Reed hospital is a military medical center in Washington, D.C., that serves mostly military and high-level federal officials and members of Congress as well. At the height of the Iraq and Afghanistan wars, the number of young, battle-injured men and women being treated there was quite high, and I knew from Joe's stay for his aneurysm how tough it could be on caregivers and their families. So, like a lot of legislators and their wives, I started visiting monthly after the inauguration.

Walter Reed is a place where too many vibrant, active people must come to terms with losing their legs or arms, and they must adjust to a life without full mobility. It's difficult to see people so young, who should be running marathons or biking around town with little kids hitched behind them, now stuck in beds. And their spouses—often caring for a newborn or toddler, just beginning their career, or finishing school—were also confined there, not willing to leave their partner's side.

At just twenty or twenty-two, patients and their partners often had to make the kinds of life-changing care decisions that people three times their age struggle with. It took a special kind of courage and strength for these wounded service members and their families to face their new realities. I can't tell you how many times I saw a couple and thought, *That's it, this tragedy is going to define them for the rest of their lives,* only to come in months later and see them not just recovered, not just beating the odds, but actually mentoring the new patients and inspiring them to get better, too.

On one of my trips, I met Brian and Brianna Mast. Brian had lost both his legs below the knee, and Brianna was coping with a new life caring for him, as well as their newborn baby boy. But from the first time I met them, just a short while after their lives had been upended by the tragedy, I could see that there was so much strength and resilience in them both. Brian was determined that he would master his prosthetic legs and continue to lead the active life he once had. Brianna was by his side through every doctor meeting, every physical therapy session. When

he seemed down——as anyone would be——she never let him stay
stuck in depression. She would wheel him down the halls of the
hospital, baby strapped to her chest, teasing him and making
him laugh. I could see by the way he held on to her hand, by the
tilt of his body toward her, by the way he looked to her when
he talked about the challenges of recovery——he was drawing so
much from her strength.

Many of the husbands and wives like Brianna have to become experts overnight——in medical advancements and navi-
gating a complicated health care system, in veteran benefits and
advocating for their spouses.

Still, while there were so many people struggling to hang on
to their health——and even their lives——Walter Reed wasn't a sad
place. You could look around and see the miracles of modern
medicine as you shook the robotic hand of a war hero. In almost
every room, you could feel the positivity and resilience of our
uniformed men and women. They refused to be defeated. They
refused to let tragedy define them.

About a year after I met Brian and Brianna, I was back visiting when I met another service member who'd lost his legs. He
told me that for a while, all he could think about was the things
he'd never be able to do again. The pain and the lost opportunities were too much, and he'd been feeling hopeless. But then,
another soldier had reached out to him and took him under his
wing. They started doing physical therapy together and playing
ball at the gym in their wheelchairs. This man was beginning to
see that his life wasn't over. Thanks to his new friend, he had
hope. And his inspiration? It was Brian.

Just a year after his own injuries, Brian was thriving. He'd
found a new mission: helping his wounded brothers and sisters

in arms move forward. It wasn't the battlefield he had imagined, but it was the one where he was needed most.

I found myself going back to Walter Reed less as a duty as Second Lady and more because I just loved spending time with these families, who felt like part of one big extended circle. Everyone there was tied together through military service in some way, and it was easy to feel a quick connection with the people I met. So, every now and then, I would get my staff and a few friends together, and we would go make dinner at the hospital.

We'd bring real tablecloths and candles—because dinner isn't dinner without candles—and make homemade food, such as chicken casserole or chili and corn bread. Sometimes we'd bring a celebrity chef along—Chef Geoff, Sunny Anderson, Sam Kass. Senate spouses and senior military spouses would join us as well. We wanted to give patients and their families some of the normal world they knew before Walter Reed, before injuries, before Afghanistan or Iraq. We wanted to bring them a piece of home.

Soon, we thought, why not just bring them home?

That first year in the administration, Kirsten White and Carlos Elizondo, two of my staff members, decided to start a new tradition on the Monday before Thanksgiving. We asked Walter Reed to give us a list of patients who were mobile enough to travel, and the hospital organized a bus to pick them up, along with their family members. We bought a couple of gigantic turkeys, and with the expert help of our staff—and our industrial kitchen—made all the fixings you could want: stuffing, mashed potatoes, sweet potatoes, cranberries, green bean casserole with crispy onions on top, and pumpkin and apple pies. We opened a few bottles of wine and made a centerpiece of gourds and pumpkins.

No matter who you are or where you come from, we are all connected through that most basic human need: food. Food, to me, is love. As the great Anthony Bourdain said, "Food may not be the answer to world peace, but it's a start." Opening our home to share a meal was the best way I could imagine supporting our fellow military families.

When our guests arrived, they were formal and often nervous at first, so Joe and I made a point to be at the front door to welcome them. They were always dressed up, ready for a serious affair; they were meeting the vice president of the United States and the Second Lady, after all. A military chaplain would open our dinner with a beautiful prayer, and everyone would begin to carefully eat. But by the end of the night, the kids were running around laughing while their parents chatted openly and grabbed second pieces of pie. In the candlelight, we were all just families, telling stories.

That first year, we invited a mother of a young man who was in a coma after having suffered a head injury from an explosion. She had planned to join us, but when her son's fever spiked, she wouldn't leave his side at the hospital. I thought about her all night, and when the final guest left, I decided we had one last errand to run. So I grabbed Carlos, our social secretary, and some of our naval aides and other staff, and we packed up the leftovers to bring to the hospital. Though most of the rooms at Walter Reed were a stark white with sanitized fluorescent lights, we found her in a dark room lit only by the yellow haze of the TV, as if her fears and anxiety over her son's health had dimmed the room around her. She took the food and hugged me without a word. Just before I turned to head back home, she smiled and said softly, "I'd like you to meet my son."

As we walked into his room, I had to stifle a gasp. His head was caved in where a piece of his skull was missing, and the skin around his eyes looked dark and sunken. I didn't need a doctor to tell me he was teetering on the edge of his life. I walked to the other side of his bed, and we stood there, fixed by the gravity of the man between us. She asked me to pray with her. We held hands over him, asking God for the miracle that would bring her son back. I didn't have to imagine her pain; I could see it in her taut mouth, her labored breath. We finished our prayer, and then I walked to her side of the bed to give her a hug. There was something between us I couldn't describe—a bond between two military mothers, perhaps—and nothing else needed to be said. I left her with her son and walked to the car in silence.

A year later, we hosted another Thanksgiving dinner. The mother I'd shared that moment with was no longer staying at Walter Reed, so she didn't join us. But someone there knew her—a handsome young man in a bright red baseball cap. He was funny and talkative and had brought a pretty young woman as his date. It wasn't until he took his hat off that I recognized him by the telltale dent where his skull was missing. He had survived the fever, the coma, and the injury and seemed to be living a healthy, mostly normal life. I hugged him and told him to say hello to his mom for me. Then I said a silent prayer of gratitude for his family.

Over the next eight years, we continued the Thanksgiving tradition and hosted barbecues in the summer and kids' Christmas parties as well. We had a special party for United Through Reading, a wonderful nonprofit that connects deployed military parents with their kids through reading. We set up a surprise gathering where a deployed father Skyped in from Iraq and read *'Twas the Night Before Christmas* to his son's second-grade class. Most of the kids in the class weren't military connected and were completely surprised to see their classmate's dad on the screen. The soldier's wife and three-year-old son were also in attendance, and when his face popped up on the screen, the little brother started shouting, "Daddy! Daddy!" His sons were proud to show off their dad to the class, while the other kids looked at this soldier like he was a celebrity. With one simple act, the worry and loneliness those kids felt for their dad was washed away by pride and love.

We kept up our tradition of eating with our troops wherever we went. In mess halls from Fort Carson to Camp Pendleton, from Berlin to Baghdad, we shared meals with the men and women who served our nation. It was a simple communion, but it connected us in a way that was deep and human—a way that felt like family. No matter where we were, we all had a way to feel at home.

For the first year of our administration, Beau was in Iraq. Though I had been working with military families in a variety of ways at that point, I now had a more personal experience with the challenges they faced, as they were playing out in my own family as well. It wasn't just that Natalie and little Hunter missed their daddy; it was that his absence changed so many things in their lives. He couldn't come to their school events, he couldn't hug them on their birthdays, and even though we Skyped as much as possible, even though the whole family did our best to make the kids feel loved and special, we couldn't fill the empty chair at the table.

After Beau came home—full of stories about the incredible men and women with whom he served and the bonds they had forged—I felt my own bond to the military community grow stronger. It came to feel like an extended military family. So in 2010, Joe and I decided to spend the Fourth of July with our troops in Iraq. We had traveled to international bases before—in fact, the previous Fourth of July, we visited a long-standing base in Berlin. But Iraq was another world altogether.

In the hostile skies of Baghdad, planes must land by flying in tight circles, like descending a spiral staircase. Pilots abruptly stop over the runway and begin corkscrewing to the ground so that it's difficult to target the plane with surface-to-air missiles. It happens distressingly fast—within around ten minutes—and when Joe and I stepped onto the tarmac, I was dizzy and completely disoriented.

An armored car took us to our accommodations for the trip: Camp Victory, a repurposed palace that had belonged to Saddam Hussein. Giant black marble columns with delicate gold details lined rooms now filled with military furniture and camo-clad soldiers running back and forth. Our room, in a sand-colored building across a pond from the large main palace, had the traces of opulence that once defined Saddam's over-the-top décor but was now filled with six spare bunk beds and a latrine. Despite the heavy heat, we decided to take a walk to see the sparkling chandeliers and intricately designed domes of the main hall. This was where Joe and General Raymond Odierno would perform a naturalization ceremony the following day for the service members deployed to Iraq who were to be sworn in as American citizens.

It was on that walk that we met a group of generals, one of

whom told me a story about his daughter back home. At his six-year-old daughter's school Christmas pageant, one of her classmates suddenly burst into tears when "Ave Maria" was played. As her teacher took her offstage and comforted her, she learned that this had been the song that had been played at her father's funeral. He had lost his life while serving in Iraq. Her teacher and her school were unaware that she was a military child.

That night, I lay awake thinking about his story. That little girl had carried a lifetime's share of grief and had grown so tough under its weight that the adults in her life didn't even know she was struggling.

I decided I wanted to do more to support kids like her—and like Natalie and little Hunter.

To my surprise, there were very few resources for how to talk about these experiences with kids. In fact, when we looked for a book on the military-family experience from a child's perspective, we couldn't find a single one. So I decided to write one.

I started by talking to Natalie—she was seven at the time and had a better understanding of what was going on than Hunter, who was just five years old—and listening to her stories. She told me about baking cookies for her dad's care package, about seeing his name on the church bulletin prayer list, and about showing her dad her loose tooth over a video call. Together, we came up with the stories that would make up a book entitled *Don't Forget, God Bless Our Troops*, a line we borrowed from the bedtime prayers we would say with the kids. It was a story of waiting, of feeling proud and sometimes sad. And it was the story of her love for Beau, and his for her. On each page, I wrote the refrain that helped her get through that year: *Be brave, Natalie.*

Michelle and I began our work with military families by traveling to bases, holding listening sessions, and meeting with experts, especially those from the military community. It was important that the spouses and kids, who knew what they needed better than anyone, lead the conversation. After we had a good grasp of the gaps that existed, we launched Joining Forces, focusing on the three issues we knew had a big impact on families: education, health, and employment.

The travel and events we did for Joining Forces—the shared experiences of sitting with people who had been through so much and listening to their stories—bonded Michelle and me in a special way. I always knew she had my back, as I had hers.

And then there were our husbands.

Both families have gotten a kick out of the memes about Joe and Barack's so-called bromance. And, while I haven't read it, I know there's now also a murder mystery novel that features the two of them. Like most good jokes, there's some truth behind it—though not the part where they're homicide detectives. But Joe and Barack are big fans of each other.

Michelle and Barack and Joe and I complemented each other in different ways, and we all brought unique talents to our professional and personal relationships. But the bottom line was that the four of us really *liked* one another. We share a similar sense of humor: sarcastic and silly. We like a good book and a great sports team. During our long hours traveling, we passed the time recounting stories about our families and making each other laugh. And Michelle and I both loved mocking our important husbands.

The Obamas are legendary in so many ways, but underneath it all, these extraordinary people were ordinary—just a family doing their best like the rest of us. Despite everything they had to think about—national security, political debates, the administration's agenda—they still made a point to put each other first. And that's exactly what Joe and I did as well.

We have a rule: no matter what we're doing, no matter what crisis we're in the middle of, if the kids call, we pick up. Whatever else we are, we are parents and grandparents first. When Ashley had a big event in Wilmington, we found a way to fit it into the schedule. My staff might have hated moving things around now and again, but they knew how important it was to me. And it wasn't just our kids—even today, when one of my sisters is sick, she'll call me for advice on which doctor to call. When she needs to be picked up, I'm the one who finds a way to get her home from the appointment. I'm the oldest, so it's always been my duty to carry on where our mom would have. Family is who we are, and we knew when we got to Washington that we wouldn't be able to leave those parts of ourselves behind.

Barack and Michelle had the same approach. Michelle's mother, the warm and loving Marian Robinson, moved with them to D.C. Both Joe and I had lost our moms by this point, and Marian became a mother figure to the two of us as well. Meanwhile, our grandchildren Naomi, Finnegan, and Maisy went to school with Barack and Michelle's daughters, Sasha and Malia. Maisy played basketball with Sasha, and Barack occasionally coached (he also once announced to the entire U.S. Olympic Basketball Women's National Team that Maisy was a "baller," which both embarrassed and delighted her). Barack and Michelle rarely missed a game, and we tried not to, either. The entire gym would be lined with Secret Service agents; staff would be there, tapping away on their BlackBerrys. And then, the Obamas and Bidens. Were we sitting in the stands like dignified public servants, composed and statesmanlike? Nope. Despite the important entourage that had to accompany us, we were out of our seats, cheering with the rest of the families.

Our lives in D.C. may have been extraordinary, but we were all trying to carve out something close to normal for our families. One of the most refreshingly normal parts for me was having friends to laugh and share adventures with. Through the good times and bad, sharing those experiences with the Obamas made us a close, blended family—one I was infinitely grateful for when everything began to fall apart.

When Beau was diagnosed with glioblastoma—a rare and aggressive brain cancer—in 2013, he didn't want anyone to know about it until we were more certain what would happen. Joe and I respected his wishes, as did Hunter and Ashley, and for months the only people who knew what he was going through were immediate family and his doctors. Eventually, though, given the time we were spending with Beau and his wife, Hallie, at his appointments and treatment, we realized we had to let Barack and Michelle know what was happening. They were the only people we told, and they were almost as devastated as we were. But they held that knowledge close. They hugged us and comforted us when they could. And Joe and I went on, living double lives as if we weren't aching on the inside at every moment.

In one of the darkest times of our lives, their friendship meant so much to us. They had become our family. And as he delivered the eulogy at Beau's funeral, President Obama reminded us of the strength of that bond:

> I will tell you what, Michelle and I, and Sasha and Malia, we've become part of the Biden clan. We're honorary members now. And the Biden family rule applies. We're always here for you, we always will be.
>
> My word as a Biden.

15

SHATTERED

Faith sees best in the dark.
—SØREN KIERKEGAARD

I believed that Beau would live. For over a year, I watched him fight his cancer. His chemotherapy was difficult. He underwent operation after operation. He had always been so athletic, so strong, but his muscles leaned over the months, and the pain was harder and harder to manage. Still, through it all, he never lost his positivity. "It's going to be okay," he'd tell me from his hospital bed. So I hoped.

I knew, deep down in my gut, that he would beat the odds. Yes, they were one in one hundred. But Beau was invincible. He was special. I felt like if I believed hard enough, if I prayed hard enough, we would all look back on his battle together. It would be another challenge we overcame as a family. I never gave up—as a mother, you can't.

I still don't have much to say about his death. Words all feel hollow. Nothing can convey what we lost. Nothing can describe the hell we found ourselves living through. At the funeral, both Ashley and Hunter spoke. I was in awe of the strength and composure of my children. Hunter was Beau's best friend and North Star, and he had led us through those terrible months, never leaving Beau's side, always there with a word of encouragement. When Beau died, I know Hunter lost his other half. But at the funeral, he stood up for all of us once again. In his beautiful speech, he addressed me and said, "You mended all of our hearts once . . . I know you will make us whole again." It's a sentiment I want badly to live up to but one that I'm not sure how to fulfill. I wish I knew how to fix a shattered family, especially when I often feel too broken to know where to start.

After the funeral, the family traveled down to South Carolina to stay at the home of dear friends on Kiawah Island. We were raw from those final weeks of Beau's illness and needed a place to recover. Wilmington had poured out love for us, and yet, the reminders of Beau were everywhere; we felt like we could never catch our breath. Everything was darkened by the shadow of his death. Even surrounded by family and friends, each of us was trapped in our sorrow. And so we gathered up the kids and grandkids and headed to the beach, hoping for some healing from the clean salt air.

While there, we followed the aftermath of the massacre at Mother Emanuel AME Church. The tragedy had taken place just an hour south of us in Charleston. We watched the heart-wrenching stories about the shooting on the news: the way the Bible study group had welcomed this killer with love; the hour they had spent with him, praying and discussing scripture; the heroism of Tywanza Sanders, gunned down at twenty-six, who tried to save his great-aunt, whose last social media post read:

"A life is not important except in the impact it has on other lives." The carnage was devastating, every detail more horrifying than the last.

So twenty days after President Obama delivered the eulogy at Beau's funeral, he traveled to South Carolina to deliver another for the senior pastor of Mother Emanuel, Rev. Clementa Carlos Pinckney, and we decided to join him.

Clem, as he was known to his friends, was just five years younger than Beau. He also served South Carolina as a state representative and then state senator. He saw no delineation between those two callings—his work was rooted in his faith and his faith was manifested in his life's work. As we walked into the convention center where the memorial was held, my heart was in my throat. We made our way to our seats, and the music of the gospel choir flooded over me, just as it had done almost a month earlier at St. Anthony's in Delaware, where we held Beau's funeral. It was hopeful: *It reaches to the highest mountain, and it flows to the lowest valley—the blood that gives me strength.* It was bittersweet: *My mother's gone to glory, I want to go there, too.* All around me was a community that had suffered so deeply, and yet, there was a sense of joy in those gathered to celebrate Rev. Pinckney's life. Their collective faith seemed undaunted, and I wished that I could share it with them. Where was my faith?

When I was growing up, my parents, self-proclaimed "agnostic realists," never took my sisters and me to church, but both of my grandmothers attended church every Sunday—Grandmom Jacobs to a Baptist church, and Ma Godfrey to a Presbyterian one. Jan, Bonny, and I would tag along on our visits, and I found I preferred Ma Godfrey's small church. I loved the dark sanctuary and glittering stained-glass windows. It was a modest chapel, but I could feel the history in the old wooden pews—the lives that were bookended there, the simple weddings and somber funerals, and all the tiny miracles in between. I loved listening to Ma sing the hymns in her strong alto: *His eye is on the sparrow, and I know he watches me.*

In junior high school, we stopped making the weekly trip to see my grandparents, and though I was happy to spend more time with my friends, I began to miss the services with Ma. So, my sophomore year of high school, I found a church just down the road from our home in Willow Grove. With a stately granite exterior, bell tower, and soaring steeple, historic Abington Presbyterian was every bit as beautiful as Ma's church. But the elegance of the building was secondary to the way I felt there. Sitting in the candlelight, listening to the doxology, taking the bread and wine—I was a part of something greater than myself. And when I prayed, I felt truly connected to God. Prayer, more than anything else, gave me a sense of peace and was something I would call upon over and over again throughout my life.

My faith has always been intensely personal and not something I spoke about often—then or now. But when Abington Presbyterian offered membership classes, I decided to take them and become an official member of the church. At age sixteen, I underwent my confirmation, and to my surprise, my mother even came to the service. And though I never encouraged it, when Jan and Bonny became teenagers, they did the exact same thing. All three of us had felt a need for spirituality in our lives.

When Beau died, Joe drew from his deep Roman Catholic

faith. It's such a big part of who he is. The Kierkegaard quote, "Faith sees best in the dark," seems to be written on his heart. Religion is his internal lantern, and he moves by its light, no matter how dark or difficult the terrain. I know a great many parents who have found solace in the church after a child's death. Perhaps it's the promise of reuniting with their loved one some bright morning. Perhaps it's the soothing idea of a plan put in place by a being who knows more than we ever could. Perhaps it's just the comfort that can be found in scripture and ritual, "a lamp unto my feet."

As Walt Whitman wrote, "Some people are so much sunlight to the square inch." Beau burned so brightly in my life that without him, I felt blinded by the darkness. I felt stuck in that void, unable to move.

One of my last true prayers was one of desperation, as Beau began to slip away from us, and it went unanswered. Since then, the words don't seem to come. The beautiful stained-glass windows I once loved, the warm wooden pulpits, the rich red kneelers—now I can see only cold colored light that refuses to shine on him, his unspoken Rosary, an empty space at the Eucharistic table.

I knew Rev. Pinckney's funeral would be difficult, but I was resolved to go. I thought of Tywanza Sanders's mother, who had watched her son die, and I ached for her. I asked myself, *What would Beau do?* And the answer was easy: he would go. His strength was a gift to me his entire life, and I knew I had a responsibility to try to be strong for others when I could. I wanted to be the mother—the person—he would want me to be. And so I thought of my own mother's steel, her fortitude, and tried my best to channel it.

No one knew that President Obama was going to sing "Amazing Grace" during his remarks. It was astonishing to hear—the raw emotion in his voice, the kindness and humility from the most powerful man in the world. In that moment, every one of us was united, in grace, in love, in allegiance against the evils that had brought us together. It was almost too much to bear, and I thought my heart might burst.

After the memorial, the President, the First Lady, Joe, and I met individually with the families of the Charleston Nine. Cynthia Marie Graham Hurd, who had managed the Charleston County Public Library; Susie Jackson, a beloved member of the choir; Ethel Lee Lance, the church's sexton; DePayne Middleton-Doctor, a pastor who helped students at Southern Wesleyan University; Tywanza Sanders, heroic twenty-six-year-old and grandnephew to Susie; Daniel Simmons, a pastor who also served at Greater Zion AME Church; Sharonda Coleman-Singleton, a speech therapist and coach at Goose Creek High School; Myra Thompson, a Bible study teacher; and, of course, Clem.

The loss of this group—this small family of believers bound by faith—left a hollow place not just in their homes or in the church but in the entire city of Charleston. It seemed their deaths, and the evil behind them, were enough to shake anyone's faith.

In small rooms, we hugged the family members. They spoke in low voices and told us stories about the lives lost. We said the things that had been said to us so often over the last month: "I'm so sorry," and "His life made a difference to so many people," and "We're praying for your family." It was hard, but there was a relief in it as well. These mothers and fathers and sisters and brothers understood the weight of our loss in a way no one else could. They knew the complicated truth of every smile we forced, every gaze we held a bit too long, every sigh we let escape. In that way, we were the same. And though we were there to comfort them, they scooped us up and held us close to their broken hearts with all the love they could give.

It felt like being lost in a lightless cave and then reaching out to find another explorer in that subterranean world. Our sorrow was cold and quiet. None of us knew how we would move forward, how we would ever get back to normal, how our families would ever heal, but at least we knew there were others down here asking the same questions, desperately searching for the strength to climb back up to the light.

Hidden in crowds, scattered throughout workplaces and grocery stores and parks, there is a fraternity of people who've lost sons and daughters. To the uninitiated, we look normal, average, whole. But like a secret handshake, I can spot them sometimes—by the sadness in their eyes or the curve of their shoulders, as if they can still feel the small arms of a child wrapping around their neck. I meet them at speeches and public events. Recently, I was getting my nails done when a woman came up to me and started to cry. I knew before she spoke. "I'm a Gold Star mom," she said, "and I just wanted to show you a picture of my son." She pulled a worn memorial card from her purse with his photo on it, and as she cried, people nearby asked uncomfortably, "What's the matter? Is everything okay?" But there's no good way to announce to a nail salon, *Isn't it clear? Our sons are gone, and we are shattered*. I just hugged her instead. And every May, on the anniversary of Beau's death, she finds a way to get a note to me. One year, she left it with a nail technician who passed it along. She recently came to one of my speeches just to support me. We share a bond that will last forever: two strangers, two mothers, with broken hearts.

Membership to this fraternity comes with no guide, and I have no advice, no wisdom to dole out to new initiates. A friend of mine lost her son, a firefighter, in a terrible blaze. He was young, with two kids, and they carried his body to the grave wrapped in an American flag. I wanted so badly to offer her words of hope or to tell her it's going to get better. But I don't know if that's true. Instead, I wrote her a note to say I was thinking about her and that she isn't alone. That's the truest thing I can say to parents who know this impossible pain: you are not alone.

Hundreds of letters poured into the White House after Beau's death, notes and cards for both Joe and me. Joe found comfort in reading the stories and looking at the photos. "The only thing we can hope for is that our children make us proud by making a difference in the world," one man wrote. "Beau has done that and then some. The world noticed." I was so grateful for the support, but I, on the other hand, couldn't read a single word. It's a subtle difference in the way we handle grief; Joe loves to remember what Beau meant to people, while I can't face the memories. I keep my letters in a bag in my closet—too precious to get rid of, but unopened all the same. They might stay that way forever. Some things you—*I*—just can't face.

There's a story that's sometimes called the parable of the long spoons. No one is sure which religion or philosophy it originates from, though it seems to appear as a myth in many traditions. The details change across cultures—spoons, chopsticks, soup, or rice. But the basic points are the same:

A man asks God to show him heaven and hell, and God presents to him two rooms. In the first, sickly people sit around a table, and in the center is a gigantic pot of delicious-smelling soup. Each person can reach the pot, but their spoons are so long that there is no way to get them back into their mouths. Each tortured soul struggles in vain to get a bite to eat. They writhe in pain as they fruitlessly ladle and starve. This, of course, is hell. And in the second room is the same table, the same soup, the same terribly long spoons—but this time, the diners, sated and happy, pour spoonfuls of soup into their neighbors' mouths. In hell, we starve alone. In heaven, we feed each other.

I know two things as I write this: I am not healed, but I am also not alone.

Over these last three years, I have been saved by the kindness of family, friends, and strangers. I have learned to lean on them when I can't stand as tall as I'd like, to let my starving heart be fed.

I now know the power of pain, to lay each of us bare, to strip away our pretenses and break down the structures we thought held us together. But I know, too, the power of compassion, like air for the drowning. I know that a gesture, even small, can become an act of mercy—a phone call, a joke among friends, an unexpected note. When you have been hollowed out, these connections, these moments of kindness are the only things that can begin to fill you. They are the only language your heart can understand.

My family is broken, but we are still holding on to each other for dear life. We are connected to this sorrow forever—to each other and to the world of fragile, hurting people around us. It is a lesson I hated to learn, but one I think—I hope—we are capable of surviving.

The grandkids ask Joe to take them to church like we used to, so, when we're in Wilmington, they go to a service together, but I stay behind. I still have a lot of unanswered questions. Where I once saw order, I now see chaos. Where I once felt that peace that surpasses understanding, I now feel hollow silence. I'm still not ready for sermons or prayers.

Every now and then, my pastor, Greg Jones, sends me an email to see how I'm doing. He understands my absence from church but regrets it nonetheless. He often says he hopes I have found a new spiritual home, to which I always have to demur. Greg recently reached out after we lost a family friend—an incredible woman who went to school with Hunter and Beau and worked with us for many years. She was just a year younger than Beau, and she left behind a loving husband and two young boys—Greg knew her death would hit close to home.

"One of my favorite quotations," I replied to his condolence email, "is 'Faith sees best in the dark'—yet sometimes it's so hard to keep believing." In his response to me, he agreed that faith is most difficult in times of trial, and yet, it was deep loss that helped him see God not as a being who works by reward and punishment, but "as the One who works slowly and quietly by love, who is with us in our suffering, who calls us to a life of love, and who urges us to work in partnership in building a new future." He reminded me of the meaning behind Kierkegaard's wisdom: that when the world goes our way, it's easy to see purpose and divine love in our lives. But it's our darkest times, the times when we have run out of hope, when there is nothing left for us to do, that we need God most. It's those times that we have to let go of reason and reach out in the blackness, believing we will find the love and comfort we need.

I'm beginning to reach out again.

I'm lucky to be surrounded by people who love me as completely as my family does. I've learned to let go of my need to be strong, and that it's okay to be vulnerable with them—in fact, it's the only way to survive. I've realized that the weight of this life is just too heavy to carry by myself at times, that we have to shoulder it together. And I know now that we can. Beau's place at our table will never be replaced, and it will never stop being mourned, but our aching hearts keep beating, keep loving, keep growing.

And one day, I hope I can salvage my faith. I'd like to be able to pray the way I once did. So many people in my life need prayers, and I feel like I owe that to them. After all, in heaven, we feed each other.

EPILOGUE

Where the Light Enters

The Monday before Thanksgiving in 2016, I stepped out of our car after a familiar drive through neighborhoods of gray-blue shingled houses and faced a cottage not far from the Nantucket Sound. The grandkids, all five of them, piled out of our rental car, laughing and teasing each other as they collected their bags. Joe unlocked the door, and I took a deep breath of the cold New England air before going in.

The year before, the family had escaped to Rome. Nantucket was just another place to remind us of all that we had lost, like a photograph with Beau's face cut out. I knew how hard it would be to come back, but this year the grandkids had asked. Thanksgiving *was* Nantucket. They missed the little shops, the ice cream parlor we always visited, the traditional Friday lunch. They wanted to watch the Christmas tree lighting and wander the cobblestone streets. They wanted to be together. To feel normal again.

So Joe and I said yes.

Inside the house, the kids picked their rooms and figured out the Wi-Fi for their phones. They pulled out all of our favorite games: checkers, cards, Monopoly. They easily fell back into our old routines. I watched Natalie and little Hunt play and wondered, as I'd wondered a million times about Hunter and Beau, how someone so young could be so strong.

Last spring, Natalie, Ashley, and I were driving home to Delaware on one of those perfect days before the mid-Atlantic humidity really takes hold. It was one of the first times I was riding with someone who wasn't a Secret Service agent, and it felt special to be really alone with my family again. All of a sudden, Rachel Platten's "Fight Song" came on the radio, and Natalie said, "Nana, turn it up!" And the three of us sang as loudly as we could, barreling down the road, zooming past the reborn trees with their tiny green buds reaching again for the sky. As I listened to Natalie belt the words, "This is my fight song / take back my life song," I remembered her resilience through Beau's deployment, and I could feel his spirit in her now. *Be brave, Natalie,* I thought.

At the house in Nantucket, we lit a fire in the fireplace, and Joe told stories about the adventures of young Beau, Hunt, and Ashley. Thursday, I set the table with fresh flowers, gourds, and candles, of course. We laid out all of the food and went around the table and said what we were thankful for. Then the grandkids' favorite tradition: the annual reading of their Christmas wish lists. "Xbox One *X,* Nana. The new one," I was directed.

As I watched the kids laugh in the firelight, I thought about that first year—me and Joe, Beau and Hunt, exploring Nantucket for the first time. It was where we learned how to be a family—all the complicated story lines of birth and death, marriage and divorce, hurt and healing, love and love and love, coming together in this little town on the edge of the world. We had formed and carried on traditions here. We had begun to rebuild here. And now, our grandchildren were doing the same.

We move forward, day by day. We heal each other, day by day. I know I am not ready to pass on this mantle—setting the table, surprising the kids on April Fools' Day, buying flowers for Neilia, making birthday dinners, and keeping these people I love more than my own life safe. I never pass up an opportunity for an embrace anymore. I grab my grandkids and hold them close like it might be my last chance.

The Friday after Thanksgiving, Joe, ever up for a challenge, woke up early to do the Polar Bear Plunge with Natalie and Maisy. After a hot shower for our swimmers, we sat by the fire and had breakfast. Later, we drove down to Main Street, where, to our surprise, the store windows were filled with signs. "Welcome back, Bidens!" they read. Someone must have heard we were coming.

That evening, we held hands in the street as the whole town gathered together. Santa himself counted down, *three, two, one,* and the giant tree in the middle of the square lit up like a star cluster. The choir sang, and we all joined in: *Silent night, holy night, all is calm, all is bright.*

I looked at Joe and smiled a real smile. As flakes of snow drifted around us, I remembered the words of Albert Camus: "In the middle of winter I at last discovered that there was in me an invincible summer."

After forty years, our legacy is resilience and loyalty and trust and hope. Yes, hope, too. How can we be hopeless when there are children around, pulling us together again, even when it's the last thing we may want? After all the pain and loss, the joy and victories, this is what we have to show: our family. These fragile lives, tied to our own through blood and choice, through love and friendship, through hardship and joy.

We are broken and bruised, but we are not alone. We rejoice together. We preserve together. We walk hand in hand through the twists and turns, and when we can't walk, we let ourselves be carried. It is the gift we give: our strength, our vulnerability, our faith in each other. We know we cannot heal ourselves, but we can lean on each other; we can lift each other up.

This is what makes us family. This is where the light enters.

ACKNOWLEDGMENTS

I originally started out to write a book of vignettes about all of the amazing people I had the opportunity to meet during my years as part of the Obama-Biden administration. These individuals and their stories had such a profound impact on me and my views on life, I wanted every reader to feel the excitement and wonder that I felt during those eight years. I was so grateful for the experiences.

Yet, my publisher wanted something more from me—what was my unique story? I thought about it for weeks, gathering stories about my life that helped to shape me. Thank you, Bob Miller, Will Schwalbe, and Sarah Murphy for loving my book as much as I did. You steered me in the right direction when I tended to get off course. Sarah, you meticulously read my manuscript and offered suggestions that were so right on point; you deserve an extra thank-you. Thank you also to Keith Hayes, Michael Cantwell, Marlena Bittner, and Nancy Trypuc for their work on my book.

Michelle and Barack Obama were great partners—we're grateful for a friendship built on love and trust. Michelle and

I worked closely together from the very beginning. I love her sense of optimism and positivity. She possesses inner strength and radiates confidence, energy, and a sense of fun. Thank you to her team, who complemented my own team in so many wonderful, positive ways. Every trip together was an adventure, an opportunity to serve our country, and it was magical to all of us. And Michelle's mother, Marian, is a favorite of both Joe and me. In many ways, she reminds us both of our mothers, and she offers us nothing but kindness and love. It is always a joy to see her.

I have to thank Team Jill, as my staff call themselves. The many women and men who worked around the clock at the White House: Cathy Russell, Anthony Bernal, Meg Campbell, Courtney O'Donnell, Carlos Elizondo, Kirsten White, Debbi Clark Bauserman, Betsy Massey Walker, Amy Laitinen, Annie Tomasini, Ashley Williams, Melanie Fonder Kaye, Paola Ramos, Sheila Nix, Sarah Baker, Houston Johnson, Julie Mason, Haley Matz Meadvin, Richard Ruffner, Michael Stennis, Kellen Suber, James Gleeson, Jamie Lyons Lawrence, Naseam Alavi Rodriguez, Teresa Jones, and Anne Marie Muldoon. And, today: Mala Adiga, Gina Lee, Jordan Montoya, Rory Brosius, Lisa Simms Booth, and Amber MacDonald.

To the men and women of the United States Secret Service, it's hard to express gratitude for all that you did for my family and me; day after day, with professionalism and integrity— always preserving our dignity in the most sensitive of times. You and your families will always have my heart.

I'd like to thank Craig Gering, Mollie Glick, David Larabell, and Kate Childs of CAA, who were my constant champions and who opened up the world of authors and publishers. They offered sage advice and counsel.

Thank you to Lisa Dickey, who listened to my stories for hours and hours and hours. She skillfully shaped the framework for all of my stories, providing invaluable perspective. Lisa is a master of her craft. Ultimately, she offered friendship, and for that I am grateful.

Many thanks for the artists, poets, and authors who allowed me to use their words to emphasize a point, thought, or emotion. As an English professor, I appreciate the power of words to touch someone's soul. Thank you to Amber MacDonald, my speechwriter, who suggested touches of beauty and poetry to my stories. Her skillful touch and her uncanny ability to put herself in my shoes added invaluable dimension to my book. She has a gift.

A special thank-you to Anthony Bernal, who spent countless hours, holidays, and weekends to push me to write. He carefully read every word, every sentence, and provided me with insights and guidance. He was invaluable in this process. He could also push me to tell my truth—my story—and he did it with unfaltering patience. He knows how much I love him and respect him.

To my mother and father, Bonny and Donald Jacobs, who provided me with the example and foundation on which to build my own family. They showed me the importance of unconditional love in so many ways. In times of strife or turmoil, I seek to hear their voices counseling me on what to do, how to handle a situation. Even in death, I hear them still. My family—and my book—reflects their love and devotion to one another and to me and my four sisters: Jan, Bonny, Kim, and Kelly.

And to you, Joe: your greatest gift to me—besides our children—was always believing in me, and therefore I believed in myself. You never wavered in your praise and encouragement. When we married, you told me that my life would never change—but it was really your love that never changed. I know I am loved.